HOW HAITI CAN MAKE THE WORLD DREAM AGAIN

Practical Ways to Champion the Transformation

JEAN RICOT DORMEUS

ISBN (Hardcover) :979-8-9987413-1-9

Library of Congress Control Number (LCCN): NRC114455

Published in the United States by Dream Again Press Silver Spring, Maryland, USA 06/06/2025

Cover and Interior Design by Dream Again Press Design Team
Printed in the United States of America

Other formats available:
Ebook ISBN: 979-8-9987413-2-6
Paperback ISBN:979-8-9987413-0-2

BISAC Codes:
- POLITICAL SCIENCE / World / Caribbean & Latin American
- SOCIAL SCIENCE / Developing & Emerging Countries
- RELIGION / Spirituality

THEMA Codes:
- JPWH – Political Science and Theory: Developing countries
- 1KJH – Haiti (Geographic qualifier)
- 5PS – Spirituality and religious inspiration
- 5PG – Social and ethical issues
- 3JM – 21st century (Time period qualifier)

First edition, 2025

To my fellow Haitians, particularly the victims of exclusion and violence, so that we remember who we are and pursue our lofty destiny in love.

I currently serve as a Staff Member of the Organization of American States (OAS).

"The content of this publication does not necessarily reflect the position or opinion of the Organization of American States, or the General Secretariat", in accordance with article 101.4(f) of the Staff Rules.

Twenty percent of the profit from every book sold will be dedicated to supporting the Movement of Prayer for Haiti (MPH), empowering initiatives for reconciliation, peace, and prosperity in Haiti.

TABLE OF CONTENTS

PREFACE

It is a great honor and privilege for me to write a review of diplomat Jean Ricot Dorméus' book "How Haiti Can Make the World Dream Again": Practical Ways to Champion the Transformation.

The book is already expected to be a bestseller. It represents an innovation in socio-political essay writing. It objectively tackles the Haitian problem, asserting that Haiti can once again become a remarkable country capable of astonishing the world anew. The content of this book is intended to motivate the reader. It optimistically and affirmatively argues that Haiti can make the world dream again. It also presents practical ways of promoting and encouraging the transformation we all dream of.

Jean Ricot Dorméus has never ceased to be the apostle of change through his writings and his various interventions in forums, local media, and social networks. In fact, all his positions have helped to make him a household name and one of a select number of apostles of change in our country.

This text is full of motivation for our compatriots in the sense that it stimulates us to expand, aim higher and bigger, and above all, persevere in the struggle to achieve great things for Haiti, despite the many obstacles we may face in such an exceptional country.

Haiti, a land of potential and resilience, has endured centuries of adversity. This book aims to revive the dream and inspire Haitians to transform the country from a place of suffering into a symbol of rebirth and renewal. As a Haitian, a citizen of the world, and a facilitator of peace and social development, the author sees the untapped potential of the country and the hearts of its people. The book explores the issues that set Haiti back and ideas and actions to promote transformation, focusing on rebuilding national identity, stability, and prosperity.

This book aims to create a peaceful and prosperous future for Haiti by exploring key issues such as building sustainable institutions, eradicating poverty, promoting peace, forgiveness and reconciliation, and harnessing the strength of the diaspora. It promotes the vision of a Haiti that dreams, realizes its full potential, and inspires the rest of the world to dream. The author's lifelong commitment to Haiti's development and well-being reflects his dedication to the country's development.

The text explores Haiti's journey, focusing on freedom, forgiveness, reconciliation, leadership, state institutions, justice, human rights, education, universal literacy, poverty eradication, self-reliance, work, productivity, innovation, environmental restoration, tourism, and harnessing artificial intelligence. It also addresses Haiti's place in the world and the importance of love in the country's development.

It's a call to adopt a new paradigm, a new vision of transformation, perfection, a different way of thinking, a different approach that can lead to a culture of excellence, enabling our beloved Haiti to astonish the world once again.

In this publication, writer Jean Ricot Dorméus encourages his readership to sow first and reap later, because a developed country, a prosperous country, a transformed territory will be to everyone's advantage, not only for Haitians in Haiti and in the diaspora, but for the international community as a whole. This book is therefore a vindication of individual awareness, commitment, and excellence, in short, for the true transformation of our homeland.

Writer and artist De Léon Daudet rightly states, "each of us can make a real and substantial difference on this planet. By committing yourself personally to a quest for consciousness, you will truly assume a leading role in the transformation of the world."

Dorméus invites us to be aware of our multiple potentialities and never to underestimate ourselves. He encourages us to be optimistic about our nation's future.

This book contains effective tools to strengthen our faith and extinguish the sparks of negative force in our lives regarding our various intrinsic capacities as divine creatures.

Writer Jean Ricot Dorméus invites us to discover this throughout the pages of this interesting essay, the fruit of long hours of reflection and bibliographical research.

I hope this book will shed light on the ideal path to follow, so that we are not afraid to dream of positivity and success, an essential element in building the New Haiti we all dream of. Was it not Shimon Peres who said on March 30, 2016: "To achieve something truly extraordinary, begin by dreaming it. Then wake up calmly and go straight to the end of your dream without ever letting yourself be discouraged."

Twenty percent of the profits from each book sold will support the Mouvement de Prière pour Haïti (MPH), which supports initiatives for reconciliation, peace, and prosperity in Haiti.

I would like to thank researcher Jean Ricot Dorméus for entrusting me with writing the preface to this crucial document, which is now accessible to a wide audience.

I hope you enjoy reading this colossal work, "How Haiti Can Make the World Dream Again: Practical Ways to Champion the Transformation," bequeathed to us by thinker Jean Ricot Dorméus, whose ideas and reflections will undoubtedly continue to move forward.

Enjoy, dear readers, and let's continue to dream and work together for the positive transformation of our beloved homeland.

Joël Lorquet, PhD
Writer and journalist

ACKNOWLEDGEMENTS

I extend my heartfelt gratitude to Sara DeGonia, whose thoughtful and meticulous editing brought clarity, coherence, and elegance to this manuscript. Her keen eye and editorial expertise have greatly enriched the final product.

My sincere thanks also go to Valerie Lacarte, whose wise counsel and insightful suggestions helped sharpen the vision and message of this work. Her encouragement added fuel to my determination to complete it.

I am profoundly grateful to Serge Bellegarde for his invaluable contributions, both in the form of constructive commentary and careful editing of the French version of the manuscript, enabling this work to reach and inspire a broader audience.

To my family, colleagues, and friends, your unwavering support, patience, and belief in me have been a constant source of strength. Whether through conversations, prayers, or quiet encouragement, you have each played a role in the journey of this book, and I deeply appreciate your support.

This work is a collective effort of minds and hearts united by a shared dream. Thank you all.

INTRODUCTION

What comes to mind when you think of Haiti? A complex history characterized by the audacity of a unique revolution and the pain of struggle or a mixture of tragedy and triumph for many? Haiti is not merely a collection of challenges or the memory of an astounding achievement; it is a land of potential, inhabited by individuals whose spirit, resilience, and capacity to dream have endured centuries of adversity. This book is about reviving the dormant dream, rekindling hope, and charting a course forward. It aims to inspire Haitians to transform the country from a place of suffering into one that serves as a symbol of rebirth and renewal.

Standing at the junction of my experience as a Haitian, global citizen, and peace and social development facilitator, I am both a witness and a participant in this journey. I have seen how much potential is unrealized inside Haiti's borders and the hearts of its people and how much they yearn for a better future. I have heard Haitians' suffering, hopes, and dreams at home and in the diaspora. I realize that the time for transformation is now.

"How Haiti Can Make the World Dream Again" is a road map rather than just a call to change. It offers practical ways to champion the transformation. These pages will explore the issues dragging us back and look at ideas and actions that can enable Haiti to make progress. We will investigate Haiti's rich and complex past as a springboard for resilience and strength rather than as a set of tragedies. We will examine the political, social, and economic avenues toward rebuilding national identity, stability, and prosperity.

Every Haitian who dreams of a better future, every diaspora individual who longs to give back, and every friend of Haiti who believes in the strength of its people should contribute to implementing the shared ideas. This book will mainly serve readers eager to craft a peaceful and prosperous future for Haiti and those seeking to understand its history.

We will explore key questions:

• How can Haiti build enduring institutions and overcome political unrest and economic decline?

• How can Haitians eradicate poverty and generate sustainable wealth?

• In a society split by years of suffering, how can Haiti experience peace, forgiveness, and reconciliation?

• How can the diaspora contribute more significantly to Haiti's rebirth, and how can we best leverage its strength?

• How can the process of Haiti's rebirth serve as a source of inspiration to its people and the world?

Every chapter helps construct the new vision and offers methods for its implementation.

"How Haiti Can Make The World Dream Again" reflects a lifetime of commitment and service to Haiti's development and welfare. I have been involved in diplomacy and international cooperation, social projects, Bible inspired spiritual support, and the unrelenting search for peace and prosperity for my country.

Join me on this adventure. Let us foster the vision of a Haiti that dreams, realizes its full potential, and inspires the rest of the world to dream.

CHAPTER 1

FREEDOM IS NOT FREE

Live as free people, but do not use your freedom as a cover-up for evil. 1 Peter 2:16

The Haitian Revolution shines as one of the most remarkable events in human history. It was the narrative of a once-enslaved people who rose against one of the world's most powerful armies, driven by an unquenchable thirst for freedom and a strong desire to regain their dignity from their oppressors. However, more than two centuries after its independence, Haiti remains plagued by toxic leadership, mismanagement, and unrest. Rather than being a symbol of success, Haiti usually languishes as "the sick man of the Americas." How has such a victorious revolution failed to inspire succeeding generations to develop a rich and stable society?

To comprehend this paradox, we must consider the reasons that propelled the Haitian Revolution and examine how they molded the country's identity. Toussaint Louverture, the revolution's most iconic leader, had a clear picture of the ideas and strategies required for true emancipation.

Despite the oppressive bans on education, Toussaint's journey revealed the transformative power of knowledge. His godfather, Father Simon Baptiste, defied colonial laws to teach him how to read and write. Bayon de Libertad, the plantation manager, further nurtured Toussaint's intellectual growth by giving him access to his library. Toussaint discovered via these acts of insubordination that the secret to escaping the bonds of physical and mental servitude was knowledge. His desire to learn was unquenchable despite the repressive system that denied him that opportunity. He discovered strength—the ability to envision freedom for his people—and knowledge in the banned books that influenced him.

In addition to military tactics, Toussaint based his leadership on unity and a shared goal. He established strategic partnerships with liberation fighters such as Henri Christophe and Jean-Jacques Dessalines, forming a mastermind that planned the only successful slave revolt in history. Their cohesive leadership achieved military triumphs and established the groundwork for fundamental nation-building ideas. This mastermind approach to leadership may teach a potent lesson for all developing nations: true transformation starts when enlightened minds work for a common and transcendent objective.

Despite being slight in stature, earning him the nickname "the walking stick" as a child, Toussaint's mind was a reservoir of strategic knowledge and philosophical thought. At sixteen, two books transformed his worldview: the History of Rome which taught him that slavery was not bound by race, and the writings of Abbott Raynal, a priest who predicted that a leader would rise from slavery in the Caribbean to lead his people to freedom. These texts ignited within him a vision that transcended his immediate circumstances. Toussaint's story became one of rebellion and intellectual liberation, embodying a truth that resonates across all movements for freedom: the mind must be free before the body can follow.

Toussaint's talent and understanding increased. Known for his capacity to lead militarily and politically, he brought together several groups under his leadership, including Black and mixed-race communities. The only thing that could match his military savvy was his diplomatic ability. He formed a unified opposition that resisted the invaders' dividing forces by arranging intricate discussions, signing treaties, and captivating escaped slaves and rebels from all throughout Saint-Domingue.

However, Toussaint was not just a hero of the military. He was a visionary and politician who saw that only a just society could guarantee true freedom. One of its era's most innovative political texts was his Constitution of 1801. It proclaimed that "all men are born, live, and die free," outlawing slavery and establishing equality, human dignity, and the unalienable right to property.

Toussaint's vision for Haiti was not merely one of independence from colonial powers but of a society where virtue and talent, not skin color or social status, would determine a person's standing.

This vision of freedom, however, was fiercely contested. During Haiti's struggle for freedom, Napoleon Bonaparte, the Emperor of France, occupied Europe with one of the strongest armies in history. France has attained previously unheard-of influence and might, with Napoleon hailed as one of the greatest military tacticians in history. The French army, well-fed, well-armed, and disciplined, seemed unstoppable. Napoleon dispatched more than twenty thousand troops, led by his brother-in-law, General Charles Victor Emmanuel Leclerc, to quash the Haitian Revolution and restore French control over its most prosperous colony.

Initially, Leclerc's forces gained the upper hand by capturing and deporting Toussaint Louverture through treachery. Nevertheless, Toussaint's spirit remained unbroken in the face of defeat. He notoriously cautioned his captors, "By overthrowing me, they have struck down the trunk of the tree of freedom for the Black; it will spring up again, for its roots are deep and numerous!" His prophetic words resonated throughout the mountains of Saint-Domingue. True to his prophecy, his removal galvanized the remaining revolutionaries under the fierce leadership of Jean-Jacques Dessalines.

Toussaint's alliances and military genius went beyond defeating enemies; they were part of a larger vision that freedom should shatter chains and secure a future where Haiti could thrive independently. His leadership eventually secured Haitian independence and served as a model for oppressed peoples around the world.

Toussaint Louverture and the Haitian revolutionaries made a lasting impact on history. Their struggle for independence exemplified the power of perseverance and strong leadership. They left lessons for the present: freedom is never given; it has to be gained. Freedom needs sacrifice, unity, moral conviction, effort, and courage to maintain.

The Haitian Revolution is a reminder that leadership must be rooted in knowledge, vision, and a love for the community it serves. Built on strategic planning, lifelong learning, and teamwork, Toussaint's leadership style is still as applicable now as it was more than 200 years ago.

However, Haiti's subsequent history begs challenging questions. Why has the country been unable to fulfill its revolutionary aspirations in the wake of such a remarkable victory? What caused the country to falter under corrupt leadership and economic mismanagement? These questions are perplexing. For Haiti to "make the world dream again," as it once did during its revolution, it must rediscover the principles that drove its birth: the unshakable belief in the value of freedom, the power of knowledge, and the necessity of collective leadership.

Toussaint Louverture organized and galvanized the revolutionary process in Saint-Domingue. Even after his deportation and death in France, his transformative vision inspired Jean-Jacques Dessalines, other generals, and their barefoot soldiers to carry on the affirmation of their dignity to its ultimate consequence: an independent Haiti.

Toussaint's achievements have inspired countless leaders around the world. On April 23, 2023, the president of France, Emmanuel Macron, paid a vibrant tribute to Toussaint Louverture on his 220th birthday and the 175th anniversary of the abolition of slavery in France:

"Toussaint Louverture embodies the triumph of will over fate. Born in slavery, but given the nature of a 'free man' in his own words . . . he knew the claw of the whip on the flesh and the pain of the cuts on the skin. He also discovered that his parents, who came from present-day Benin, had been separated at the time of their enslavement. He experienced, as an orphan of a mother, the violence of slavery, which destroys all dignity and replaces the bonds of the family with the chain of masters. Toussaint Louverture transformed this condition into ambition. Because nothing ever frightened him.

The gallop for inspiration, sovereignty over his pace and movements, he was already free. He was born a slave but became a child of the Enlightenment. Brilliant autodidact, discovering Diderot, Raynal, learning the art of war with Plutarch. By conviction, as by temperament, he refused all assignments.

An exceptional revolutionary, Toussaint Louverture also believed that only order could maintain freedom, prosperity, and the public good. The order of discipline and military rigor to mix former slaves, natives of Africa, brigadiers of color, and French officers within his army. The order of citizenship he had established, where everyone had to serve with probity and humanity. The order of the laws he had promulgated to tame passions, interests, and arbitrariness. The order that awakened the minds in the schools that Toussaint Louverture had built allowed progress, thanks to the hygiene that he promoted, to the teaching of the arts that he favored. It is the order that guaranteed freedom, the order married to effective freedom which alone makes it legitimate, that of the Republic itself.

For this reason, Toussaint Louverture is a hero. [Charles Maurice de Talleyrand-Périgord] said of men, they are statues: you must see them in place. Thus, Toussaint Louverture has imposed himself in our collective memory, and that statue is unmovable.... Yes, Toussaint Louverture was a Republican, as army chief and statesman. Against the racist prejudices of the time, he demonstrated to whoever doubted it that these despised slaves, considered less than men, could surpass the soldiers of the most powerful nations of Europe. 'Does the color of my body harm my bravery?' he asked.

Toussaint Louverture had never failed in his duty to humanity. Against those of his people who intended to take revenge on the whites of Saint-Domingue, he saved, amnestied, and sought harmony. . . . Toussaint Louverture defended the rights of whites, of blacks, of all. . . . He evaluated the quality of men not by color but by greatness. He intended to build a new Nation based on equality, fraternity, friendship, and progress. In short, a universal Republic." [1]

Relevant knowledge, strategy based on a common goal, and leadership working in harmony and trust were key principles that guided the impressive success of the indigenous army, despite being ill-equipped and deprived of advanced technology. These principles flowed from the love of Toussaint and his lieutenants for the community of slaves from which they emerged. They witnessed the indignities handed down by the colonizers, including the destruction of families, the raping of girls and women, cruel executions, forced labor in inhumane conditions, and denial of education. They felt the responsibility to reclaim dignity for their people, inspiring them to overcome their fear of punishment or execution. Love for their brethren mobilized their creativity, courage, and strength.

The revolution's story is not just Haiti's. It is a story of human potential, a testament to the idea that no force on Earth can stop a people united in their quest for dignity and justice. The time has come for Haiti and the world to reconnect with this powerful legacy and apply its lessons to the present.

Toussaint Louverture and other revolutionary leaders in Saint-Domingue (Haiti's name before independence) did more than outmaneuver the armies of Spain, Britain, and France; they forged a movement grounded in the ideals of liberty, equality, and fraternity. Inspired by these ideas, arising from the French Revolution, they turned their fight into one of global importance. Remarkably, despite tremendous odds, these freedom fighters used

---

[1] "Prononcé le 27 avril 2023 - Emmanuel Macron 27042023 Abolition de l'esclavage en France | vie-publique.fr."

their convictions as weapons to show that the desire for justice and dignity could overcome even the most sophisticated armed forces.

Under the leadership of Dessalines, Toussaint's successor, the revolutionary forces delivered a final, decisive blow at the Battle of Vertières in 1803. They defeated the mightiest military power of the time and secured Haiti's place in history as the unique nation born from a successful slave revolt. In addition to shattering the bonds of slavery and colonialism, the victory rocked Europe and the Americas, upending the fundamental tenets of white supremacy and imperialism. To remind their adversaries of the common ideals they had previously fought for, the Haitian soldiers, many of whom had once been slaves, chanted the French Revolutionary anthem, "La Marseillaise," during battle. The stirring cries echoed across both sides' ranks:

"Arise, children of the Fatherland,
The day of glory has arrived!
Against us, tyranny's
Bloody standard is raised."

The song made the French soldiers face an unsettling reality: the people of Saint-Domingue were being denied access to the very principles they had fought to uphold in Europe. Their spirits suffered because of this moral inconsistency. They started to doubt the morality of their goal. Their bewilderment and uncertainty undermined their determination and reduced the potency of their better weapons.

General Christophe, one of Toussaint's most important supporters, mocked the French soldiers' hypocrisy of singing about liberty while battling to restore slavery[2], as historian Eric A. Gordon pointed out.

The irony was not lost on the Black revolutionaries, who turned the anthem into a subversive declaration of their right to freedom. Similarly, as historian John Newsinger recounts, upon hearing the revolutionary song sung by the enemy, a French soldier

[2] Gordon, "The 1802 Haitian Revolution on Stage."

lamented, "I sang that song across Italy and Austria. . . . Can you tell me, Major, what have we come here for?[3]"

Armed with more sophisticated weapons and a reputation for military superiority, the French army found itself undermined by the sheer moral power of the Haitian revolutionaries. Toussaint, Dessalines, Christophe, and their compatriots had a cause that transcended material advantages. They fought for their humanity, dignity, and right to exist as free people, not for conquest. Their moral clarity gave them bravery, tenacity, and an unquestionable belief in their success.

One of the biggest military shocks of history resulted from the conflict of values between the French army and the Haitian liberation fighters. The revolutionaries won despite their contrasting looks, degrees of readiness, and access to resources. Equipped with justice and resolve, the lesser force overcame one of the most formidable military forces, much like in the biblical narrative of David and Goliath.

General Leclerc's death in 1802 signaled a turning point as General Donatien de Rochambeau's surviving French forces battled to restrain the indigenous army's increasing force and will. On November 18, 1803, the revolutionary forces defeated the French at the final Battle of Vertières. This triumph was more than just a military one; it was a turning point in human history marking the end of colonial rule and the start of a new era of freedom for the slaves.

An army of once enslaved people had vanquished their colonial masters on the battlefield for the first time in recorded history. This triumph established an example for other conquered countries and dealt a fatal blow to the transatlantic slave trade, therefore felt globally. The chronicles of freedom and justice bear permanently the names of Dessalines, Christophe, Alexandre Pétion, François Capois, Marie- Jeanne, Lamartinière, and other Haitian leaders.

[3] "Liberty and Equality in Haiti."

The terms of the French surrender at Vertières reflected the respect the Haitian officials possessed—even toward their adversaries. Recognizing the compassion of their opponent even after years of terrible conflict, the treaty let the last French forces safely leave. Showing a degree of compassion seldom seen in the aftermath of such a horrible fight, the Haitian generals guaranteed the sick and injured French soldiers would be cared for until they could return home.

Triumphant Haitian leaders declared Saint-Domingue's independence on January 1, 1804, renaming it Haiti as in the native indigenous tongue.

This move not only restored the dignity of the Black population but also sent a strong message to the world: no country, no matter how strong, could permanently deny a people their right to freedom and self-determination.

The notion that military strategy and power by themselves assured the success of the liberation fighters has only surface appeal. Behind the military strategies were the real drivers: a burning desire for freedom, knowledge acquisition, cohesion within the leadership group, and, most importantly, love for kin and fellow slaves. This important lesson seems to have escaped generations of Haitians who tend to apply force, violence, or a hardline attitude to resolve national issues. Psychologist Abraham Maslow perfectly described this cognitive bias: "If the only tool you have is a hammer, you tend to see every problem as a nail.[4]"

The leaders of the Haitian Revolution used military strategy and force against a foreign entity in self-defense, motivated by deep-seated values and a belief in human equality. The widely spread idea in Haiti that threats, force, and violence would solve political and social issues may stem from a misleading interpretation of the revolution's success. This idea has resulted in a scorched-earth approach to situations that require dialogue and

[4] Ellis, "If the Only Tool You Have Is a Hammer, You Tend to See Every Problem as a Nail."

compromise.

Since gaining its independence, Haiti has endured the terrible effects of this strategy. Political leaders have attempted to uphold the social structure and advantages by neglect or coercion without addressing the need for inclusion, equitable treatment, and equal chances. The outcomes—economic decline, social unrest, and political instability—are telling. Political leaders should adopt Dale Carnegie's timeless maxim to achieve better results: "A drop of honey catches more flies than a gallon of gall.[5]" Thus, they would induce peace and social harmony, uplift the people, and sustain a culture conducive to progress.

In addition to inadequate policies, external hostility and pressure wreaked havoc. Proslavery countries joined forces to make the slave victory a bad example. The countries dominating the international scene not only isolated Haiti but also ensured that Haitians wouldn't have a chance to work for themselves, having to pay installments on a bogus debt. They forced Haiti to ingest a disease agent that slowly shriveled its chances of development. By doing so, they wanted to show that the cost of liberty was too high and prevent any enslaved group from attempting to emancipate itself.

The Eddie Murphy and Dan Aykroyd film Trading Places provides a powerful allegory for Haiti's crushing under the weight of the independence debt and outside forces. The affluent Duke brothers in the movie control the lives of two men as part of a vicious experiment, simulating how foreign powers have dominated Haiti's future and economy.

France's imposition of a hefty reparation debt in 1825 damaged Haiti's economy following its independence, much like the protagonist Louis Winthorpe III, who goes from privilege to poverty at the whim of outside forces. This debt robbed the country of potential wealth and strengthened poverty and foreign rule.

---

[5] Carnegie, How to Win Friends & Influence People.

The Duke brothers' manipulation is representative of how Haiti's colonial overlords and later international forces manipulated the country's destiny to retain control and stifle its independence. External forces that mimic the fabricated manipulation of the characters' circumstances in Trading Places include trade embargoes, political interference, and the crushing independence debt.

Similar to how the individuals in the film were maintained in socially manufactured environments, foreign exploitation methodically hampered Haiti's development and wealth creation prospects. The film ultimately shows how the power dynamics are based on manipulating resources and opportunities, reflecting the external forces that have historically manipulated Haiti's destiny for profit.

CHAPTER 2

AFTER THE DANCE, THE DRUMS ARE HEAVY

It doesn't matter where you came from. All that matters is where you're going.[6] *Brian Tracy, writer and motivational speaker*

On January 1, 1804, Haiti became the first free Black republic in the world and has since held the record of the only successful slave revolt in the history of humanity. As Jean Ziegler would say, "the rebels against the world order"[7] won the victory. Haiti's newfound sublime chords of liberty have reverberated around the world. The downtrodden of the earth received with delight the echo of this music and started their liberation waltz to its rhythm.

Indeed, the Haitian Revolution changed the course of history. Before Haiti's independence, soldiers from Saint-Domingue, known as the Chasseurs-Volontaires, in 1779 teamed up with the US forces at the Battle of Savannah. This group included twelve-year-old drummer Henri Christophe, who became King of Haiti.

The Haitian American Historical Society organized a monument to honor the unsung heroes of the US freedom movement—the Haitian soldiers who fought in the brutal siege of Savannah during the Revolutionary War—on October 8, 2007, 228

[6] OBE, ""It Doesn't Matter Where You Came From. All That Matters Is Where You Are Going" Brian Tracy."

[7] "Amazon.Com: Les Rebelles: Contre l'ordre Du Monde : Mouvements Armés de Libération Nationale Du Tiers Monde (L'Histoire Immédiate) (French Edition): 9782020064132: Ziegler, Jean: Books."

years after that battle. The memorial statue was unveiled at Franklin Square in Savannah as a tribute to these soldiers who had played a significant role during the Revolutionary War and acknowledged the support they gave to the founding of the United States.

The global significance of Haiti's independence cannot be overstated. Dr. Bertrhude Albert identified five compelling reasons why the world took notice of Haiti's extraordinary achievement:

Expanding the Meaning of Freedom: Haitians were the first to extend the idea of freedom to include people of color under the law. While the American Declaration of Independence (1776) and the French Declaration of the Rights of Man and Citizen (1789) were revolutionary, neither fully embraced the idea that slavery and racial discrimination were grave violations of human rights. Haiti broke this barrier, setting a radical new precedent for liberty.

Catalyst for the Abolition of the Slave Trade: Only three years after Haiti declared independence, Britain abolished the transatlantic slave trade in 1807. This was no coincidence. Haiti's success in overthrowing French colonial power inspired a wave of abolitionist movements. Thomas Clarkson, a leading British abolitionist, leveraged Haiti's example to strengthen his case against the slave trade, eventually leading Britain, and later the United States, to pass legislation to end this horrific practice.

The Louisiana Purchase: Haiti's revolution directly influenced one of history's greatest real estate deals, the Louisiana Purchase. Even with his vision of building a vast French empire in the Americas, Napoleon Bonaparte was forced to abandon this ambition when the Haitian Revolution weakened France's foothold in the Western Hemisphere. Haiti's wealth as the "Pearl of the Antilles," producing vast amounts of sugar and coffee, was key to France's prosperity. However, when the French lost control of Haiti, Napoleon agreed to sell the Louisiana territory to the United States, thus doubling its size.

A Haven for Freedom Seekers: After gaining independence,

Haiti became a sanctuary for former and current slaves seeking refuge. The revolution inspired other liberation movements throughout the Caribbean and the Americas. Haiti even provided financial and moral support to revolutionaries like Simón Bolívar, who led several Latin American countries to independence. The striking resemblance between the flags of Venezuela, Colombia, and Ecuador to Haiti's flag is a testament to Haiti's influence on the liberation of Latin America.

Resilience in the Face of Oppression: Despite achieving independence, Haiti was forced to pay France an enormous indemnity of 90 million francs (equivalent to US $21 billion today) to be recognized as a state. These reparations were a crippling burden, taking Haiti over a century to pay off. Furthermore, the country faced international isolation, with nations like the United States refusing to recognize or trade with Haiti for decades. Yet, through all these adversities, Haiti endured, standing as a symbol of freedom and resilience.[8]

Dorbrene E. O'Marde, vice chair of the CARICOM Reparations Commission, highlighted Haiti's significant contributions—physical, human, and ideological—to the wars of independence in Central and South America between 1808 and 1826, when Spain lost all its American colonies except Cuba and Puerto Rico.

Venezuela is perhaps the most prominent example of Haiti's influence. General Alexandre Pétion, then president of the Republic of Haiti (1807–1818), is revered as the father of the Pan-American movement. His unwavering support for the liberator Simón Bolívar, which included the provision of weapons, ammunition, and Haitian freedom fighters, came with two conditions that reflected Haiti's staunch anti-slavery stance. The first condition was that Bolívar must abolish slavery in an independent Venezuela and any future liberated countries in South

[8] "5 Reasons Why You Should Care About Haiti's Independence Day (January 1st)."

America. The second was that any enslaved individuals captured by privateers must be sent to Haiti, where they would be granted their freedom.

Haiti's commitment to freedom was enshrined in Article 44 of its 1805 Constitution, which declared that any Black person or indigenous individual who arrived on Haitian soil would be immediately recognized as free and granted citizenship. Haiti even went so far as to offer captains of slave ships payment for their human cargo, not to enslave them but to set them free.

Historical records demonstrate that thousands of Africans, brought on slave ships from the United States, Latin America, and the Caribbean, found refuge and freedom on Haiti's shores, solidifying the nation's role as a beacon of liberty in the hemisphere.

France officially recognized Haiti's independence in 1825, but only in exchange for a crushing indemnity. The sum imposed on Haiti was ten times the amount the United States paid France for the Louisiana Purchase, which doubled the size of the US. Haiti, a newly independent nation, was forced to take out loans from a French bank at exorbitant interest rates to compensate former French slaveholders for their "lost property.[9]"

Professor Marlene Daut aptly describes this debt as *"the greatest heist in history.*

" In 2017, Forbes estimated that the indemnity, adjusted for modern value, amounted to $21 billion. Shockingly, the US took an interest in Haiti's finances, receiving payments related to the indemnity. By 1922, much of Haiti's debt to France had been transferred to American investors, extending Haiti's financial burden. It took the nation 122 years—until 1947—to fully repay this unjust debt and the massive interest it accrued.

The idea of former slaves paying reparations to their oppressors is staggering. Marlene Daut explains, "Surrounded by French gunboats, a newly independent Haiti was forced to pay its slaveholders reparations. It

[9] Rojas, "BATTLE OF VERTIÈRES."

was the former slaves of Haiti, not the French slaveholders, who were compelled to compensate their oppressors and their descendants for the privilege of being free."[10]

In a powerful address at a special session of the Permanent Council of the Organization of American States on November 4, 2015, the Right Honorable Ralph E. Gonsalves, prime minister of St. Vincent and the Grenadines, vividly described the astronomical ransom imposed on Haiti. He explained, *"By 1825, twenty-two years after the death of the Haitian revolutionary leader Toussaint Louverture, the Haitian army was weakened and divided. France exploited this vulnerability, threatening to re-enslave Haitians if they did not comply with a demand for 150 million francs and a 50 percent tariff reduction for all French ships docking in Haiti. To meet the first payment of 30 million francs, the Haitian government was forced to borrow the full amount from a private French bank, MM Ch Ternaux Grandophe et Cie."*

After further negotiations in 1838, the French-Haitian Treaty of Friendship reduced the original obligation from 150 million francs to 90 million francs. However, Haiti was still required to make annual payments of at least 2 million francs for thirty years, alongside repayment of the original loan. Thus, Haiti was coerced into taking out additional loans to satisfy an outrageously unjust demand.[11]

The independent life experience faced continuous hostility, isolation, and strategies from pro-slavery governments to contain or reverse the march of freedom. In the face of such a predicament, the nascent national journey oscillated between inspiring militancy for freedom and difficulties in organizing functioning institutions and an effective public administration. Haiti oscillated between efforts to revive the worn-out war economy and attempts at redistributing wealth, between deprivations due to international isolation and policies to reinvigorate the agriculture and export sector, and between unity against slavery and social polarization.

---

[10] Rosalsky, ""The Greatest Heist In History.""
[11] "OAS :: Speeches."

The cadre of managers and professionals who could have piloted the transition to a stable political and social system either fled the country or were decimated. The victorious army was the only vibrant institution standing. So, the generals and other military leaders had to shoulder the burden of ruling and administering the new nation, a role for which they had not been prepared. Therefore, a culture of improvisation, on-sight navigation, cronyism, and compulsion set in. The nation-building exercise reeled from the long-term impact of these negative forces on society. Therefore, Haiti has not found the right track for political stability, social harmony, and economic progress.

For more than two centuries, the early flaws in Haiti's national foundation have haunted its leadership and people. These flaws were worsened by repeated foreign interventions, which drained the country's resources and stunted its development. Besides France and the United States, other global powers, such as Spain and Germany, exerted pressure on Haiti as seen in the Admiral Rubalcava and Lüders affairs.

In 1861, Dominican Republic President Pedro Santana invited Spain to reassert control over the eastern part of Hispaniola, and in return, he was offered the position of governor-general. Independence-minded Dominicans resisted this move, taking up arms to defend their freedom. Spain held Haiti responsible for this resistance and dispatched a fleet led by Admiral Rubalcava to threaten Port-au-Prince with bombardment. Though the matter was ultimately resolved without violence, this episode highlights the risks Haiti took to support liberation movements and the fear colonial powers had of Haiti's influence as the successful slave revolution.

The Lüders affair of 1897 further illustrates the external pressures Haiti faced. German businessman Emil Lüders, involved in an altercation with police in Port-au-Prince, was sentenced to one year in prison. The German government intervened, demanding Lüders' release. When Haiti resisted, the US mediated, leading to his release. However, Germany escalated the situation, sending warships to Port-au-Prince and demanding twenty thousand dollars in damages, an apology, and a twenty-one-gun salute to the German Empire. Due to a lack of international support and military strength to resist, Haiti was forced to comply with these humiliating demands.

One of the most significant foreign interventions in Haiti was the nineteen-year US occupation. In their article, Haiti's Troubled Path to Development for the Council on Foreign Relations (CFR), Rocio Cara Labrador and Diana Roy added: *"The United States recognized Haiti only in 1862 when President Abraham Lincoln was championing emancipation at home and abroad."*

US Marines landed in Port-au-Prince on July 28, 1915. Within six weeks, American representatives had taken control of Haitian customs and administrative institutions. For the next nineteen years, the United States essentially governed Haiti, with Marine Corps commanders acting as provincial administrators and wielding veto power over Haitian governmental decisions. At that time, a staggering 80 percent of Haiti's government budget was drained to service debt owed to French and American banks.[12]

Haiti resisted the American occupation from the start. Though some Haitian politicians collaborated with the occupiers, many Haitians joined the "Cacos" resistance fighters. Leaders such as Charlemagne Péralte and Benoît Batraville became symbols of this resistance. Péralte was assassinated, and Batraville was executed for his defiance. Other anti-imperialists, like Rosalvo Bobo, were forced into exile.

The US left behind some infrastructure, including roads, bridges, telephone systems, schools, and hospitals. However, the US administration also imposed racial segregation, denying dark-skinned Haitians leadership roles in public administration. This imposition limited the transfer of skills and knowledge needed to develop the nation.

An article published by GlobalSecurity.org titled "Occupation

[12] "Haiti's Troubled Path to Development | Council on Foreign Relations."

of Haiti (1915–34)" states:

By 1930, President Herbert Hoover had become concerned about the effects of the occupation, particularly after a December 1929 incident in Les Cayes in which marines killed at least ten Haitian peasants during a protest against local economic conditions. Hoover appointed two commissions to study the situation...

One of them, the Forbes Commission, praised the material improvements brought by the U.S. administration but criticized the exclusion of Haitians from positions of real authority in the government and the Garde d'Haiti (Haitian military). The commission further noted that *"the social forces that created instability remain: poverty, ignorance, and the lack of a tradition or desire for orderly free government."*[13]

Seven Haitian presidents had been deposed or assassinated before the occupation. The United States maintained control over Haiti's security and finances for nearly two decades. Racial segregation, forced labor, press censorship, and the deposition of presidents and legislatures that opposed US rule were part of the occupation's legacy. Uprisings against the US administration, including revolts in 1919 and 1929, resulted in the deaths of approximately fifteen thousand Haitians. In 1934, President Franklin D. Roosevelt implemented the Good Neighbor Policy, which resulted in the withdrawal of US troops.

Haiti's path remained turbulent in the twentieth century. In 1991, Jean-Bertrand Aristide became president, but political polarization and violence soon led to a coup. At the initiative of the US and the Organization of American States (OAS), an oil embargo was imposed on Haiti for three years to pressure the restoration of democracy. This embargo crippled the economy and further exacerbated Haiti's social and economic woes. Aristide was eventually restored to power in 1994 following a US military intervention, backed by a UN peacekeeping mission that remained

[13] "Occupation of Haiti (1915-34)."

in Haiti until 2000.

Aristide was reelected in 2000, but an armed rebellion in 2004 forced him into exile again. Another international force, sanctioned by the UN, entered Haiti to restore order. This peacekeeping mission lasted until 2017, marking thirteen years of international intervention.

The history of Haiti evokes the powerful Greek legends of Prometheus and Icarus.

Prometheus disobeyed Zeus by taking fire from the gods and giving it to humans. Enraged, Zeus sought to punish him. He created Pandora and sent her to Earth with a jar, instructing her never to open it. Yet, driven by curiosity, Pandora lifted the lid, unleashing evils, diseases, and suffering into the world. Zeus further condemned Prometheus to endless suffering. He was shackled to a rock on Mount Caucasus, where an eagle gobbled his liver every day, only to rebuild it overnight, continuing the cycle of agony. Prometheus' torment was eventually ended by Zeus's son, Hercules, who required help to complete one of his Twelve Labors: retrieving the golden apples Hera had gifted to Zeus. With his father's reluctant consent, Hercules killed the eagle, thus freeing Prometheus.[14]

Hope is said to have emerged from Pandora's jar as a balm to the evils unleashed. Hope persists, even when all else seems lost.

Haiti, like Prometheus, ignited the flame of freedom for the slaves and oppressed of the world. In retaliation, she has endured an onslaught of evils, foreign interventions, internal strife, poverty, and isolation as punishment for its audacity. Yet, despite the darkness, hope has never faltered. Just as Prometheus's deliverance was inevitable, so too is Haiti's rebirth. The world still needs Haiti's legacy as a reminder: no price is too high for freedom, and no dream is unattainable when people are truly free.

The second myth that parallels Haiti's journey is the legend of Icarus, which captured my imagination in the early 1980s when I

[14] "Prometheus."

watched the film I as in Icarus. This movie, inspired by the assassination of President John F. Kennedy, follows the murder of a president in an unnamed Western country by a sniper. As in the real story, the main suspect dies under suspicious circumstances and is declared the lone perpetrator. However, prosecutor Henri Volney refuses to accept this explanation and digs deeper, eventually uncovering a vast conspiracy. As he draws closer to the truth, Volney realizes he risks facing a fate similar to Icarus, who paid the ultimate price for flying too close to the sun.

The myth of Daedalus and Icarus serves as a potent allegory. An exceptional inventor, Daedalus made wax and feather wings to escape from Crete, where King Minos had imprisoned them. Daedalus warned Icarus not to fly too close to the sun, but in his exhilaration, Icarus ignored the caution. The sun's heat melted the wax that held his wings together, and Icarus plummeted into the sea.[15]

Imperialist powers viewed Haiti's independence as a direct affront. How could former slaves, once the bedrock of their economic wealth, dare to challenge the world order by glorifying freedom and human rights? Determined to see Haiti fail, these powers took turns conspiring with domestic agents to destabilize the country, slowly but surely melting its wings. For a long time, Haiti has been in free fall, spiraling from one crisis to another.

Yet Haiti's fall holds the seed of future triumph. Every failure carries within it the potential for success. Haiti's wings, though clipped, will grow back. In time, Haiti will rise again, soaring higher than ever, and its story of resilience will inspire the world anew.

The aftermath of the Haitian Revolution presented excruciating challenges. As Professor Bob Corbett wrote, *"The country was in shambles. Most of the plantations were destroyed, many skilled overseers were gone (either dead, in hiding, or having fled for their lives because of the treatment of slaves), skilled managers were often also gone, the former slaves did not want to work someone else's plantation, there was a grave fear*

[15] "The Myth of Daedalus and Icarus."

that France would re-invade, and the rest of the international community was either openly hostile or uninterested in Haiti."

When Haiti declared independence on January 1, 1804, it faced an uphill battle. The economy was in disarray, with the landscape reduced to ashes and debris. Tens of thousands of cultivators and soldiers had perished in the fight for freedom. Where once there were homes and bustling plantations, only small plots of coffee and food crops indicated any signs of life. The once-thriving sugar mills were demolished or reduced to charred ruins.[16]

The agricultural management structure had collapsed, and the newly freed peasants were unwilling to return to the plantations they had been forced to toil on. They sought ownership of their land, complicating efforts to revive agriculture. Furthermore, Haiti's leadership was improvised, leading to divisions, infighting, and rivalries that hampered governance. The military dominated the disorganized administrative system, and the education sector was virtually nonexistent and needed reinventing.

At the same time, the Industrial Revolution was transforming the global economy, and Haiti found itself unable to participate in these advancements.

Jean-Jacques Dessalines and the other leaders of the new nation faced the monumental task of building a country from the ashes, managing a devastated economy, and remaining vigilant against the ever-present threat of foreign invasion. The zeal that had driven the revolution now needed to be redirected toward implementing liberty, equality, and fraternity—and generating prosperity for all. Unfortunately, the leaders' policies put the country on a slippery slope.

The controversial theory of spontaneous generation, that a new thriving society would emerge from the void, proved unsustainable. The scorched-earth tactics used during the revolution, including the destruction of plantations and the killing of colonial leaders, resulted in the loss of essential management knowledge and disrupted the means of production. The old,

[16] "Haiti:The Post-Revolutionary Period:1804-1820."

unjust system had been dismantled, but a new economic, social, and political order had yet to be designed and implemented.

Furthermore, the culture that had developed during centuries of exploitation and subjugation was not conducive to an orderly environment. The free citizens resented work, associating it with the horrors of slavery, and their belief systems had been profoundly disrupted. After the dance and glory of independence, the drums of rebuilding were unbearably heavy. The external environment was openly hostile, and internally, Haiti struggled with the complex task of social inclusion and nation-building.

Jean-Jacques Dessalines led Haiti to become the world's first Black republic in 1804, declaring himself Emperor Jacques I shortly afterward. He implemented a strict military regime to secure the nation's independence, nullified French land agreements, and divided the population into soldiers and laborers. His governance style, which included forced labor and land confiscations through various decrees, alienated the populace and prominent mulatto landowners. These policies ultimately undermined his rule, leading to his assassination in 1806 and the subsequent division of Haiti into two regions under separate leaders, setting a precedent for recurring instability.

Following Dessalines's death, Haiti struggled with unstable governance, caught between authoritarianism and anarchy. Attempts to establish strong institutions through successive constitutions failed to build a stable political system or effective public administration. With frequent leadership changes, Haiti was unable to implement lasting reforms. The result was a long-standing cycle of ineffective governance and social unrest that impeded the country's development and the establishment of sustained democratic rule.

In the fall of 2022, at a meeting of the Permanent Council of the Organization of American States (OAS), Haiti's permanent representative formally requested international support to confront gangs and address the pervasive insecurity and violence that have afflicted the country for decades. Ambassador Léon Charles, having twice served as director general of the Haitian National Police (PNH), including during the assassination of President Jovenel Moïse on July 7, 2021, was perhaps the most qualified official to address the issue of national security.

Ambassador Charles offered a sobering historical account of Haiti's political landscape. He highlighted that, in Haiti's 218 years of independence, fifty-nine leaders have governed the country, thirty-six coups d'état have occurred, and five presidents have been assassinated while in office. Only six presidents have completed their terms.

Additionally, one head of state committed suicide, six died in office, and many others either spent only a few months in power or ended their lives in exile—notably, only a few held office for a prolonged period. Jean-Pierre Boyer ruled for twenty-five years, from 1818 to 1843, and the father-son Duvalier dynasty lasted twenty-eight years, from 1957 to 1986. Ironically, those leaders who completed their terms did so under foreign occupation or with foreign military forces present. These statistics expose a deep-seated pathology at the heart of Haiti's governance and social systems.

CHAPTER 3

HIGHLIGHTS OF HAITI'S JOURNEY

There's no way to become great overnight, but in the marathon of success, it takes a lot of intention to see you through each day of the journey.[17] *Lewis Howes, writer*

Despite facing countless challenges, Haiti has demonstrated a remarkable ability to rise, adapt, and contribute meaningfully to the global community. The country has left an indelible mark on the world, from its critical role in supporting liberation movements across Latin America to its unique cultural influence in literature, art, and cuisine.

Since its independence, Haiti has championed the cause of freedom worldwide. The country stood in solidarity with Simón Bolivar's quest for independence in South America, providing ships, soldiers, money, and weapons to aid. In 2021, Venezuelan Chancellor Jorge Arreaza celebrated Haiti's 217th anniversary of independence with these profound words: "From Venezuela, we celebrate the 217th anniversary of the independence of Haiti, convinced that the nation that is the mother of freedoms in Latin America and the Caribbean will shine again, bringing light and hope of freedom to the oppressed of the world."[18] These lines beautifully acknowledged Haiti's pivotal contributions to the global fight for freedom and emancipation.

---

[17] Howes, The School of Greatness.

[18] "Canciller de Venezuela Conmemoró El Aniversario 217 de La Independencia de Haití."

Haiti is home to one of the largest fortresses in the Americas, the Citadelle Laferrière, one of the most impressive symbols of Haiti's resolve. This fortress is located atop the nine-hundred-meter Bonnet à l'Évêque mountain, several kilometers inland. From this strategic vantage point, Haitian forces could monitor nearby valleys and the coastline, ensuring a defensive stronghold. Completed in 1820, the Citadelle has withstood numerous earthquakes. Often referred to as the "eighth wonder of the world," the Citadelle was built under the reign of King Henri Christophe to defend against a potential French invasion. It was ingeniously designed with massive cisterns and storehouses to sustain five thousand defenders for up to a year. In 1982, UNESCO designated this fortress a World Heritage site[19], cementing its place as a global landmark.

Historian Patrick Delatour noted, *"The massive effort on the Citadelle, along with two dozen other mountaintop forts, by a nation that was internationally isolated and recovering from devastating wars, could only be explained by the determination of the former slaves 'never to return to the plantation.'"*[20] This statement highlights the indomitable spirit of Haiti's people, who built these fortifications as symbols of their resolve to remain free.

Another key achievement in Haiti's history was the architectural transformation of Port-au-Prince during the bicentennial celebration of its founding. This event, known as the Festival of Peace, not only showcased the nation's rich cultural heritage but also put Haiti on the global tourism map. Historian Georges Corvington, in his book Port-au-Prince au Cours des Ans (1743–1950), documented the grandeur of this world fair.

> *Planning for the event began in March 1948, and in just over a year, the city's landscape was dramatically transformed. The event cost*

[19] "National History Park – Citadel, Sans Souci, Ramiers - UNESCO World Heritage Centre."
[20] Farah, "HAITI'S TURBULENT BIRTH HAUNTS CRUMBLING FORTRESS."

Haiti more than $4 million out of a national budget of $13.4 million, a substantial investment that paid off as many of the buildings from the exposition became permanent fixtures in the city. These included the presidential pavilion, the tourist pavilion, the post office pavilion, the agricultural pavilion, La Fontaine Lumineuse, and the Théâtre de Verdure. The event's success elevated Haiti's standing in the region, positioning it as a leader in Caribbean tourism.[21]

During the inauguration of the international exposition, President Dumarsais Estimé captured the country's forward-looking vision, stating, "The soul of the Haitian people is marching toward the discovery of a greater destiny. The desire for perfection and total renewal pervades our people, announcing that a springtime of new life and flowering is surely ahead." This sentiment reflected a broader national optimism that sought to redefine Haiti's place in the world.

Another architectural wonder, Haiti's National Palace, was admired across the Caribbean for about a century. The devastating earthquake of January 12, 2010 destroyed that elegant building. Haitian king Jean-Pierre Boyer established the first palace, the Palais de l'Exécutif, in 1820; nevertheless, it was demolished amid political unrest in 1869. Over the next few decades, Haiti's government sought an appropriate national house for its president. Still, attempts were greeted with disappointments, including structural damage caused by natural or man-made disasters. In 1912, the government hired Georges Baussan, a well-known Haitian architect educated in France, to build the new National Palace. Baussan's vision was influenced by neoclassical architecture, a style that symbolized grandeur, order, and power and was widely used for governmental buildings worldwide at the time.

The new National Palace, completed in 1920, quickly became one of the most iconic landmarks in the Caribbean. It was an architectural masterpiece that symbolized Haiti's past and future

[21] Smith, Red & Black in Haiti.

with its unique white façade, graceful domes, and classical columns.

The Haitian culture is dynamic and resilient. In his foundational work, Ainsi parla l'Oncle, Jean Price-Mars portrayed Haitians as people who "sing, suffer, mourn, laugh, dance, and accept fate" while criticizing the nation's upper class for their elitism. Haiti's culture is a blend of European and African traditions, influenced by French colonization and the experiences of enslaved Africans.

Nemours Jean-Baptiste invented the Compas (or Kompa) genre in the 1950s, making it an essential addition to Haitian music worldwide. Compas modified traditional Haitian rhythms with elements of jazz, merengue, and other Caribbean sounds, making them more accessible to a broader audience. The danceable beats, accompanied by guitar and horn melodies, swiftly spread throughout the Caribbean, Latin America, and the Haitian diaspora, making it a popular choice for social events and festivities.

Compas served as a cultural bridge between Haitians in the diaspora and their motherland, promoting cultural interchange with surrounding countries, particularly those in the French Caribbean. The genre impacted the development of Zouk, a popular music form in the French Antilles, demonstrating Haiti's musical impact on the Caribbean region.

Through performers such as Wyclef Jean of the Fugees, Haitian music has influenced worldwide music trends. His blend of hip-hop, reggae, and Haitian rhythms introduced Haitian music to international audiences.

Haitian literature is a rich facet of the nation's cultural heritage, with numerous thinkers and writers leaving an indelible mark on the world. From early pioneers to the Indigenist movement and the "Generation de la Ronde," Haitian writers have drawn from the country's deep history, folklore, and traditions to shape their visions of life and society.

Prominent figures who made significant contributions include Etzer Vilaire, Jacques Roumain, Louis Boisrond-Tonnerre, Oswald Durand, Louis-Joseph Janvier, and Anténor Firmin. More recently, Dany Laferrière's writings have blazed a trail, leading to his admission to the French Academy.

Haitian plastic arts, too, have attracted global audiences. In the mid-nineteenth century, Emperor Faustin Soulouque founded the Imperial Academy of Arts, which produced notable artists like Numa Desroches. In 1944, Dewitt Peters established the Centre d'Art in Port-au-Prince, sparking a surge of artistic expression. The center influenced artists such as Wilson Bigaud, Philomé Obin, Hector Hyppolite, Castera Bazile, and Rigaud Benoit, who achieved global fame for their unique and expressive styles.

Haitian arts and crafts are known for their bright originality, cultural symbolism, and exceptional craftsmanship, making them a valuable cultural export throughout the Caribbean. Haiti's rich artistic traditions, deeply rooted in its history and African heritage, are expressed in various forms, from intricate metalwork to vivid paintings, handwoven textiles, and carved wooden sculptures. These art forms have preserved Haiti's cultural identity and played a crucial role in supporting regional tourism.

Haitian artisans in the Dominican Republic, Jamaica, and Antigua and Barbuda have gained visibility in markets, galleries, and festivals, attracting tourists looking for authentic Caribbean experiences. The attraction of Haitian crafts, with its vivid colors and enthralling themes of history and daily life, gives these tourist destinations' cultural offerings a distinctive taste. Made from discarded materials like oil drums, Haitian metal sculptures are well-liked and demonstrate creativity and environmental sustainability. Due to this arts and crafts-based cultural exchange, Haiti and its neighboring Caribbean countries now have closer social and economic relations.

Haitian art has gained popularity in international art galleries and festivals across the Caribbean, including the Caribbean Festival of Arts (CARIFESTA), where Haitian artists showcase their work. These venues promote Haitian culture and support the tourism economy by attracting art collectors, historians, and tourists interested in Caribbean culture. Haitian paintings with rural settings and historical connections attract viewers and leave enduring effects.

Haitian cuisine has gained international recognition, and dishes such as black rice and lalo (jute leaf legume) have received accolades from various communities. In 2021, at the initiative of Ambassador Dominique Dupuy, Permanent Delegate of Haiti to UNESCO, Haiti's famous "soup joumou", a pumpkin soup historically reserved for slave owners, was included in UNESCO's List of the Intangible Cultural Heritage of Humanity. Following the country's independence, the soup became a symbol of freedom, consumed on Independence Day as a reminder of the resilience of the Haitian people.

In addition to its cultural influence, Haiti has made significant contributions to world governance and cooperation. The country was a founding member of the United Nations and the Organization of American States (OAS) and actively participated in international diplomacy and regional development. Over time, the government has supported peacekeeping missions and promoted freedom and human rights globally. Despite setbacks, Haiti has remained a voice for peace and regional stability, demonstrating its dedication to global solidarity and collaboration.

Haitians have made significant contributions to anthropology and other sciences through groundbreaking research and by offering unique perspectives shaped by Haiti's complex history and culture.

In "On the Equality of the Human Races" (1885), Haitian intellectual Anténor Firmin masterfully responds to the racist theories of Arthur de Gobineau, who advocated the superiority of the white race. Firmin methodically deconstructs these ideas using scientific, anthropological, and historical arguments, demonstrating the futility of racial hierarchies and affirming the intrinsic equality of all human races. With this visionary work, he places Haiti at the heart of the global intellectual debate, reaffirming the country's role as a bastion in the fight against racism and the defense of human dignity.

One of the most prominent figures is Jean Price-Mars, often considered the father of Haitian ethnology. His early twentieth-century work challenged colonial narratives and promoted the value of African heritage in shaping Haitian identity.

Price-Mars emphasized the importance of Haitian folklore and oral traditions in understanding the nation’s cultural fabric. His anthropological approach gave voice to the lived experiences of ordinary Haitians, contributing to a deeper understanding of how African traditions were preserved and transformed in the Americas. Price-Mars’s scholarship influenced Haitian intellectuals and reshaped global discourse on race, identity, and culture in post-colonial societies.

Haitians played a pivotal role in the Négritude. This literary and ideological movement emerged in the 1930s as a response to colonialism, seeking to reclaim African cultural identity and celebrate Black heritage. Haitian intellectuals, along with famous leaders from French-speaking countries like Martinique's Aimé Césaire and Senegal's Léopold Sédar Senghor, helped shape the movement's philosophy and expansion.

Jean Price-Mars was one of the most prominent figures in the Négritude movement. His early campaign for recognizing African cultural elements in Haitian society opposed the Eurocentric perspectives that had hitherto dominated post-colonial states. Price-Mars believed that the African origins of Haitian culture, including traditions, were essential to the country's identity and urged academics to embrace them.

His ethnological approach to understanding Haitian society inspired generations of writers and thinkers to explore African heritage as a source of strength, which became a core tenet of the

Négritude movement.

Jacques Roumain, a novelist and poet, also upheld Négritude. His novel Gouverneurs de la Rosée (Masters of the Dew[22]) is considered a classic of Caribbean literature. Roumain focuses on rural life, social justice, and cultural identity while honoring Haitian peasant customs and African history. It explores the interconnectedness of race, class, and culture.

Haitian writers like René Depestre continued this tradition, using literature to explore the Black experience and challenge colonialism and racism.

These Haitian intellectuals shaped the Négritude movement, transforming Black identity, culture, and pride in Francophone countries and beyond. Their contributions enriched the movement's philosophical foundation and offered a unique perspective grounded in Haiti's history of revolution, resilience, and cultural synthesis.

Haitians have also excelled in various scientific fields, often working on issues directly related to the well-being of their communities. For example, Haitian physicians and researchers have achieved significant advances in public health and tropical medicine. Dr. Jean William Pape, a renowned infectious disease specialist, has helped fight HIV/AIDS in Haiti. His organization, Gheskio, has led research and treatment for HIV and other infectious diseases, advancing global awareness of these health crises. Dr. Pape's research and clinical work have saved countless lives and set a precedent for community-based health interventions in resource-limited settings.

In international relations, Émile Saint-Lot played a pivotal role, particularly as one of the key figures in the international struggle for human rights. A prominent lawyer, journalist, and politician, he became Haiti's first ambassador to the United Nations. He is best known for his instrumental role in advocating for the 1948 Universal Declaration of Human Rights.

---

[22] Roumain, Masters of the Dew.

As a delegate on the UN General Assembly's Third Committee, he collaborated with world leaders to ensure the inclusion of language emphasizing the equality of all human beings, regardless of race, religion, or gender. His passionate advocacy for human rights and anti-colonialism reflected Haiti's long-standing commitment to freedom and justice, rooted in its revolutionary history. His contributions helped shape the global conversation on human rights and reinforced Haiti's legacy as a defender of universal human dignity on the world stage.

Gérard Dorcély made profound contributions to Haiti's development through his visionary leadership as the founder of the Institut National d'Administration, de Gestion et des Hautes Études Internationales (INAGHEI), an institution that has played a pivotal role in shaping Haiti's diplomacy, public administration and management professionals. He molded a new generation of leaders with the know-how to strengthen governance and promote sustainable development in Haiti.

As foreign affairs minister, Dorcély exemplified diplomatic excellence for Haiti, enhancing its relations with other countries and playing its role as a valued member of the international community. As minister of national education, Dorcély was instrumental in advancing educational reforms, promoting access to higher learning, and improving the quality of education across the country. His legacy, spanning education, public administration, and diplomacy, remains invaluable in Haiti's intellectual and institutional progress.

Emmanuel Fritz Longchamp made significant contributions to Haiti's diplomatic and international relations through his roles as permanent representative to the United Nations and minister of foreign affairs. As Haiti's permanent representative to the UN, he worked tirelessly to elevate the country's voice on the global stage, advocating for Haiti's interests in areas such as sustainable development, technical cooperation, and peacekeeping efforts.

Longchamp's diplomatic acumen helped foster stronger

relationships between Haiti and many stakeholders in the international community, particularly during political and social challenges. As minister of foreign affairs, Longchamp continued to strengthen Haiti's foreign policy, playing a crucial role in promoting regional cooperation with the Caribbean and Latin America while also seeking to improve bilateral relations with key partners. As a result of his leadership in both roles, Haiti became more active and involved on the international scene.

Another important factor in increasing Haiti's impact abroad has been the diaspora. Prominent individuals from Haitian communities overseas have raised Haiti's profile internationally in various disciplines.

The Haitian diaspora has been a powerful influence in changing people's opinions of Haiti and showcasing its potential for innovation and brilliance, from scholars and writers to politicians and businesspeople.

Haitians have made major contributions to social development, politics, culture, and education in nations worldwide. They have significantly impacted the world stage, whether teaching in newly established African countries in the 1960s, leaving their mark on North American cities like Montreal, New York, and Miami, or reshaping international organizations. The contributions of Haitians and those of Haitian descent demonstrate their capacity to bring about constructive change wherever they live.

Haiti was crucial to the post-independence development of African nations when they broke free from colonial bonds. These new countries needed government frameworks, educational programs, and infrastructure that could empower their citizens after centuries of European dominance. Given their common history of colonization and oppression, Haiti stepped in to help. Haitian professionals—especially professors and teachers—traveled to African nations like Senegal, Ivory Coast, and Congo.

This migration of Haitian intellectuals to Africa was seen as a way of repaying a historical debt of solidarity among oppressed peoples. It was also an opportunity to reaffirm Haiti's identity as a nation of freedom fighters. Haitians understood the value of education in breaking the chains of oppression and sought to equip newly independent African nations with the intellectual tools needed for nation-building.

Many of these Haitian teachers stood out for their dedication to their African pupils and for promoting a close cultural bond between Haiti and Africa. They contributed to bringing Haitian literature, philosophy, and culture to African audiences, strengthening the ties between Africa and Haiti. Many of the leaders these Haitians taught went on to assume important positions in their nations, contributing to Africa's intellectual and political growth after independence. As a result, the legacy of this educational help is still felt today.

Since the 1960s, when Haiti's political upheaval prompted waves of migration, a flourishing Haitian community has called Canada, especially the province of Quebec, home. As soon as they arrived, Haitians made important contributions to the nation's politics and culture.

The twenty-seventh governor-general of Canada, Michaëlle Jean, is among the most well-known individuals. Jean was born in Port-au-Prince, but during the Duvalier tyranny, she and her family emigrated to Canada.

As governor general, Michaëlle Jean broke barriers as the first person of Caribbean descent to hold the position and as a symbol of the potential for integration and success within Canadian society. Her tenure was marked by a strong commitment to social justice, particularly in defending women's rights, marginalized communities, and immigrants.

Additionally, Michaëlle Jean served as the first female secretary general of the International Organization of La Francophonie (OIF) from 2015 to 2019. Throughout her time in office, she worked to advance democracy, human rights, and economic cooperation among the Francophonie's eighty-eight member states and governments. Jean advocated for empowering youth and women, especially in developing French-speaking nations, and worked to strengthen cultural and linguistic ties within the global Francophone community. Her leadership elevated the visibility of La Francophonie as a platform for addressing critical global challenges, including education, climate change, and sustainable development.

The Haitian influence in Canada is also deeply felt in the cultural sector. In Montreal, home to one of the largest Haitian diasporas, Haitian culture is a vibrant part of the city's identity. Haitian Canadian writers, artists, and musicians have enriched Canada's multicultural landscape.

Haitians and persons of Haitian heritage in the US have significantly contributed to education, medicine, politics, and the arts. Haitians have gained prominence in the US political environment. In 2021, Karine Jean-Pierre, a daughter of Haitian immigrants, became the first Black woman to serve as White House press secretary. Her success demonstrates the growing impact of the Haitian community on American politics and administration.

Edwidge Danticat, a Haitian American author, has utilized her platform to share the tales of Haitian immigrants, highlighting their tenacity and challenges in both the US and Haiti. Her works, such as The Farming of Bones and Brother, I'm Dying, have earned acclaim and sparked important conversations about identity, migration, and memory.

Legendary figures such as the drummer Raymond Baillargeau better known as Ti Roro, the singer Martha Jean-Claude, Maurice Sixto, Frankétienne, and Languichatte have substantially influenced the Haitian culture. Maurice Sixto, a renowned social commentator and storyteller, employed his sharp intellect to expose social injustices through recorded monologues and spoken-word performances. Frankétienne, a literary giant, was the first to pioneer the concept of Spiralisme, a literary movement that encapsulates the fluid, cyclical character of Haitian storytelling, blending orality with the written word. Languichatte, the esteemed comedian and radio personality, popularized satirical humor by employing his performances to reflect and critique social conventions. These figures exemplify Haiti's literature and performing arts richness and power to educate, entertain, and challenge the status quo.

Haiti's journey, from the audacity of its revolution to its profound contributions to the arts, education, and global diplomacy, is a testament to the resilience and creativity of its people. Throughout history, Haiti has continually risen above hardship, offering the world a unique blend of cultural richness, intellectual prowess, and an unyielding spirit.

Haiti's potential remains vast. The nation's cultural heritage, art, music, cuisine, and traditions continue to generate inspiration at home and abroad. The contributions of the Haitian diaspora in fields as diverse as medicine, education, politics, and the sciences further amplify Haiti's impact on the world stage. These global citizens, deeply connected to their roots, bring new ideas, innovation, and hope to Haiti's unfolding story.

Haiti still has a long way to go. The nation owes it to itself to reassume its position as a symbol of hope because of the expectations it generated and its rich cultural heritage. Haiti will rise above its current difficulties and forge a brighter future. The light of Haiti's rich history continues to shine brightly, illuminating the path to a new dawn of progress, unity, and prosperity. Despite the current chaos, the world can look to Haiti with hope, knowing its best chapters are yet to be written.

CHAPTER 4

A NEW BEGINNING FOR HAITI

Moun ki bezwen deyò chache chemin pòt (Dreams don't work unless you act). Haitian proverb

From the interminable crossing of the dark and desolate valley of slavery, Haiti rose to the majestic heights of achieving the unique successful slave revolution and being the first Black republic in history. Diplomatic strategy, political astuteness, and inspiring feats of bravery followed the violent, degrading, and vile treatment slaveowners had dealt to their Black fellow human beings. Haiti's founding fathers came out victorious over the onslaught of inhumanity and cruelty that had flowed from discrimination, cupidity, and desire for dominance.

The long night of imposed despair and feeling of doom and gloom ended with sunshine that sent out rays of hope to other oppressed communities. The dream for freedom and dignity finally culminated following harrowing struggles and hardships. Then came the nagging question, "Where would the new nation go from there?" Would the vision, determination, and total surrender to the cause of freedom sustain the fresh experience of self-rule?

Haiti faced the impressive challenge of staying alert to defend and maintain freedom while crafting and implementing a vision to build and organize the new nation. The scars of slavery and war served as a reminder that the focus of the nation should not stray from but stay put on the prize of freedom, even more so as the then-dominant world powers had ganged up to nip the emerging national experience in the bud and make it a bad example. Isolation and crushing external political and economic pressures joined hands with domestic political carelessness and malfeasance in the context of a growing addiction to disorganization and destruction.

Current superpowers have sought to stop speaking the double language of justice and equality for all while subjugating other people or communities. They have realized that exploitation and domination by force and violence cannot guarantee lasting peace and progress. They have realized that slavery, segregation, and discrimination also debase those who practice these vices. They have also realized that prohibition from learning and personal development and forcing large groups of people into ignorance and mental darkness deprive politics, science, economy, and culture of needed skills and geniuses that remain latent.

In this context, now is the time to overcome the obstacles and mental blocks from the past and fully engage in the permanent process of building an attractive future for Haiti. Now is the time to redesign society, plug the gaps in its foundation, and seriously intensify nation-building[23]. Now is the time to stop looking backward and begin defining a lofty vision of the place of Haiti in the world. Haiti's progress in social inclusion, political culture, and economic development levels must, at last, keep the promises of freedom and the iconic victory for emancipation from slavery and mental alienation.

The Haitian Revolution shows that success and victory belong to those who believe, nurture a burning desire, and take action even when facing an impossible task in appearance. The genius of Toussaint Louverture drove him to develop himself, forge a vision, and make a pathway to freedom in the middle of the hostile wilderness of slavery. He has inspired numerous generations to climb and reach the top of apparently impregnable mountains of self-esteem-crushing domination. Since the successful landmark

[23] Acemoglu and Robinson, Why Nations Fail.

revolution Toussaint had pioneered, many other leaders rose and broke the yoke of social injustice and systemic discrimination that have robbed countless communities and individuals of their hope and dignity. Among these heroes, Nelson Mandela, Martin Luther King Jr., and Mahatma Gandhi stand out.

When I was an advisor to the assistant general of the Organization of the American States, Ambassador Albert Ramdin used to exhibit the portraits of Mandela, King, and Gandhi in his office. Not only did he get inspiration from these visuals, but his staff and guests could also fathom the results of belief, self-development, and commitment to a cause. These values helped Ambassador Ramdin complete two successful terms as assistant secretary-general, rise to the position of minister of foreign affairs of Suriname, and make history for the Caribbean by getting elected secretary-general, a first in the annals of the OAS.

Those three inspiring statesmen, human rights advocates, and promoters of peace through nonviolent means left their mark on the destiny of our world.

Until 1990, many devotees of human rights expressed disappointment and frustration as they observed how a majority of Black people found themselves in exile in their own land in South Africa due to the apartheid regime. Years of UN sanctions didn't seem to root out the evil of segregation in South Africa. Nelson Mandela paid a high price for freedom and social justice by languishing in jail for twenty-seven years. When he stepped out to freedom on February 11, 1990, Mandela taught the world a priceless lesson. He embraced his former abusers, brought peace to South Africa through nonviolent means, and became the first president of the transformed South Africa.

Mandela embodied resilience. He refused "to satisfy his thirst for freedom and social justice by drinking from the cup of bitterness and hatred." He refused to nurture animosity toward his jailers, realizing that evil cannot eradicate evil. Only love can unbolt hate; only light can dissipate darkness. By answering the call to stand for freedom and justice despite trials and tribulations, Mandela gave profound meaning to his life and inspired countless distraught people worldwide. As psychologist Viktor Frankl said, *"Ultimately, man should not ask what the meaning of his life is, but rather he must recognize that it is he who is asked."*[24] The name of Mandela will always resonate throughout the ages as a symbol of selflessness and courage.

Nelson Mandela was inspired by the incredible life of Martin Luther King Jr. and his leadership in the struggle for freedom and equality in America.

In a sense, King Jr. was the David who knocked down the powerful political, social, and economic Goliaths. For centuries, no force had been able to bring down the high mountains of segregation and legal discrimination. It would seem that white people felt superior by keeping down people of color through unjust laws, police brutality, exploitation, and little or no access to education.

After President Abraham Lincoln issued the Emancipation Proclamation, Black people crossed the exit gate from slavery empty-handed, with limited skills and crushed self-esteem. Every effort was made to make them believe they didn't measure up and could only remain subservient to others. When Rosa Parks refused to give up her seat on the bus, she was nowhere near thinking that her gesture could trigger the most transformative movement in America.

Rosa Parks's arrest on December 1, 1955, triggered the bus boycott in Montgomery, Alabama, and gave momentum to the civil rights movement. Martin Luther King Jr. provided leadership to the movement and, through trials and tribulations, channeled the energies of the Black community to justice and equality for all while advocating nonviolent means. His "I Have a Dream" speech in Washington, DC, on August 28, 1963, marked a watershed in the struggle for racial justice in America and the world. It took the civil

[24] Frankl, Winslade, and Kushner, Man's Search for Meaning.

rights devotees many long years of persecution, jail, and suffering—in other words, an uphill battle until they reached the bright day of the abolition of segregation and the passing of the Civil Rights Act of 1964 and the Voting Rights Act of 1965.

Martin Luther King Jr.'s wisdom, faith, and courage sustained the civil rights journey through thick and thin. Because of his determination, he overcame fear, threats, and excruciating challenges, even within his own camp.

The philosophy he expressed in the following words gave impetus to his engagement:

> *And I say to you this morning, that if you have never found something so dear and so precious to you that you will die for it, then you aren't fit to live. You may be thirty-eight years old, as I happen to be, and one day some great opportunity stands before you and calls upon you to stand up for some great principle, some great issue, some great cause, and you refuse to do it because you are afraid; you refuse to do it because you want to live longer; you're afraid that you will lose your job, or you're afraid that you will be criticized or that you will lose your popularity or you're afraid that somebody will stab you or shoot at you or bomb your house, and so you refuse to take the stand. Well, you may go on and live until you are ninety, but you're just as dead at thirty-eight as you would be at ninety! And the cessation of breathing in your life is but the belated announcement of an earlier death of the spirit. You died when you refused to stand up for right; you died when you refused to stand up for truth; you died when you refused to stand up for justice.*[25]

Such a philosophy, coupled with the nonviolence principle, delivered America from the evil of segregation and racial injustice. I stand in awe at the achievements and worldwide influence of Martin Luther King Jr. His greatness spoke to me when I visited his memorial at the Washington, DC, Mall, stood by his imposing statue, and read a quote from him engraved on the stone: "Out of the mountain of despair, a stone of hope." This hope has equipped many individuals and communities worldwide and

[25] "From the Pulpit to the Heart | King's Last March | APM Reports."

inspired them to climb their own mountains despite the appearance of unrecoverable fatality. As the Holy Scripture says in Mark 9:23: "Everything is possible for one who believes."

Martin Luther King Jr.'s journey was inspired by the achievements of Mahatma Gandhi, who is well known for his nonviolent resistance philosophy. Gandhi's twenty-one years of professional life as a lawyer in South Africa connected him with the plight of the Indian and Black communities. He also suffered from segregation and discrimination and was imprisoned on several occasions. There, he started developing the nonviolence strategy. Upon his return to India, he engaged in politics and sought to emancipate his people from British rule through nonviolence.

It may be difficult to comprehend how a seemingly bland political attitude such as nonviolence could have such far-reaching consequences. As counterintuitive as it appears, it helped Gandhi organize his people, transcend religious factions, stand against wars, and promote values that sustain peace and progress. Further, it brought an end to the British rule in India. Gandhi's influence has reverberated throughout the world, showcasing the effectiveness of the nonviolence strategy as a powerful moral and political weapon at the disposal of the downtrodden of the earth.

On the occasion of Gandhi's 150th birthday in 2019, author Nish Acharya published an article in Forbes magazine titled, "Mahatma Gandhi At 150: Lessons On Leadership." Acharya listed three leadership traits that made Gandhi a role model for the most successful political movement leaders of the twentieth century. He wrote:

Arguably, Gandhi's greatest leadership trait was his ability to visualize the qualities of a successful, post-Independence Indian nation and maintain a life-long focus on the four intertwined challenges that he believed must be collectively addressed for India to succeed. The four challenges, or goals, as articulated by Ramchandra Guha in his book Gandhi, The Years That Changed

The World were: to free India from British occupation, to end untouchability, to improve relations between Hindus and Muslims, and to make India into a self-reliant nation, economically and socially.

A second element of Gandhi's leadership was his lifelong commitment to achieving that intertwined vision of a successful Indian nation. Starting in the 1890s with his work in South Africa until he died in 1948, Gandhi wrote, mobilized, and preached about the same goals of freedom, inclusion, harmony, diversity, and empowerment. Today, few of the most committed social entrepreneurs have the energy to stay engaged on the same set of issues for 50–60 years.

Gandhi's most well-known, and most-studied, leadership trait was his willingness to live like the majority of Indians that he sought to help, and his exhortation that all Indians "be the change they wish to see in this world" . . . Gandhi was able to maintain the support of India's upper caste Hindus and industrialists while maintaining the trust of the rural and poor majority of Indians that he sought to help.[26]

Walking in the footprints of Toussaint Louverture, these three leaders, Nelson Mandela, Martin Luther King Jr., and Mahatma Gandhi, showed that willpower and commitment triumph over fatalism. No situation is so overwhelming that it can forever resist accountability, a burning desire for change, and courage. Regardless of the number of citadels and violence protecting a social order, enlightened and servant leadership finds a way to lift the torch of justice and fraternity.

The influence of these luminaries continues to ripple through the ocean of social struggles and to highlight the power of hope, especially when hope is pursued with audacity.

The audacity of hope[27] evokes the campaign of Barrack Obama as he was running for US president. His slogan, "Yes, we

[26] Acharya, "Mahatma Gandhi At 150."
[27] Obama, The Audacity of Hope.

can," galvanized large swaths of the electorate as he charted a course to victory against all odds.

In 2005, Jacob, a Caribbean-American handyman I had met in Baltimore, tried to convince me that the United States of America was not ready for an African American president. He pointed to the systemic discrimination, the historic deprivations and injustice, and the political hypocrisy, which have kept millions of Black people in the pit of poverty and have pushed them into the claws of the criminal justice system and the jails.

Jacob said that the Emancipation Proclamation issued by Abraham Lincoln took the Black community from slavery into second-class citizenship through the practice of segregation. To him, the Civil Rights Movement led by Martin Luther King Jr. had improved the situation of African Americans with the elimination of signs such as "for whites only" and the Jim Crow Laws. However, America still had a long way to go until every citizen, regardless of their skin color or social condition, could sit together on equal footing at the table of brotherhood.

At that time, Jacob could not conceive the fulfillment of the dream that a Black president could emerge from the American creed that *"all men are created equal and are guaranteed the inalienable rights of life, liberty, and the pursuit of happiness."*[28] Like Jacob, many people had become cynical and had lost faith in the unlimited possibilities at the disposal of every man or community, even in the face of crushing circumstances.

Nevertheless, Obama emerged victorious in the 2008 presidential election and was inaugurated as the first Black president in the annals of American history on January 20, 2009. The 44th president of the United States had been in office for less than eight months when he won the Nobel Peace Prize for his "extraordinary efforts to strengthen international diplomacy and cooperation between peoples." This exceptional feat proclaimed, if necessary, that no obstacle can stand forever against the power

[28] "Declaration of Independence US Constitution."

of faith and the audacity of hope.

I realized the extent, scope, and reach of Obama's victory when my friend Yves Rody Jean traveled from Haiti to attend the historic swearing-in ceremony. Rody told me he wouldn't miss the event for anything in the world because a miracle had happened. With my youngest daughter, Lynn Carla, I took the metro with Rody to the Mall in Washington, DC. Huge crowds came from all over the world to witness the celebration of a dream come true. A wave of positive energy and excitement engulfed vulnerable communities because, once more, it was proven that "nothing is impossible to those who believe."(Mark 9:23) Obama won the presidential race twice and successfully ran the US government for two terms, thus showing that humankind's only limitations derive from limiting beliefs.

Several countries in the world have recognized and celebrated Obama's landmark victory. More than sixty elements have been named after Obama in countries such as the US, Spain, Kenya, Tanzania, and Antigua and Barbuda, including species, animals, schools, streets, topographical features, facilities, and holidays. When I arrived in Antigua and Barbuda in 2010 as the Organization of American States (OAS) representative, Boggy Peak had just been renamed Mount Obama. As in the case of the Haitian Revolution, the simple act of uttering the name Obama conjures up the power of hope to overcome any apparent fatalism and a whole range of game-changing possibilities.

History has taught us that no seemingly desperate situation lasts forever. It takes leaders such as Gandhi, Mandela, King Jr., and Obama to kindle the people's faith in their God-given abilities and power.

The situation in Haiti will remain a catch-22 until the leaders of Haiti believe otherwise. Change will show up as soon as they take themselves seriously, embrace their responsibility, and nurture a burning desire for social transformation, political stability, and economic progress. Back in the late eighteenth century, the slaves in Saint-Domingue were in a worse situation than the present-day Haiti population. The will of those slaves to break free from slavery and the leadership of Toussaint Louverture performed an unprecedented feat leading to victory over the then most powerful army in the world and the birth of the first Black Republic. Therefore, Haiti can learn lessons and draw inspiration from her history to create the conditions for long-term peace and progress based on timeless principles and values.

Author Napoleon Hill made some bold statements about the power of faith and desire to bring about transformation. Here are three of the most powerful examples:

> *Helen Keller became deaf, dumb, and blind shortly after birth. Despite the greatest misfortune, she has written her name indelibly in the pages of the history of the great. Her entire life has proved that no one is ever defeated until defeat has been accepted as a reality.*
>
> *There is a difference between wishing for a thing and being ready to receive it. No one is ready for a thing until he believes he can acquire it. The state of mind must be belief, not mere hope or wish. Open-mindedness is essential for belief. Closed minds do not inspire faith, courage, and belief.*
>
> *Nothing is impossible to the person who backs desire with enduring faith.*[29]

Toussaint Louverture built his leadership upon the principles of faith in the victory for freedom against combined powerful forces. Obviously, the nation of which Toussaint Louverture is the precursor shouldn't lose faith in its lofty destiny to the point of throwing up her hands and going adrift.

The magnitude of Haiti's descent to hell conceals an unprecedented opportunity to repeat Toussaint Louverture's achievements and rebuild a better republic on sounder foundations. Every failure brings with it the seeds of an equivalent success. This principle points to the extravagant achievements to which Haiti can aspire when she gets her act together. Such

[29] Hill and Pell, Think and Grow Rich.

achievements require visionary leadership to help the country take responsibility for its development, believe in itself, embrace the values that have brought prosperity to many nations, and change its culture—all this with justice, equity, and social inclusion. Haiti can turn her condition into an ambition to reinvigorate the positive energy of the nation for progress and prosperity.

In a report for the secretary-general of the United Nations in January 2009 titled "Haiti: From Natural Catastrophe to Economic Security," Paul Collier of Oxford University wrote:

"Haiti is classified as a 'fragile state.' Yet compared to other fragile states, its fundamentals are highly propitious. If the international community cannot succeed in Haiti, it is hard to see it succeeding elsewhere." Among the propitious fundamentals, Collier listed:

A favored region. Haiti is in a zone of peace, with proximity to the United States and other stable countries.

A political window. "The political system is fractious, and so decisions are very difficult. . . . There are, of course, powerful forces for inertia. Still, while these would severely impede any wide-ranging agenda for public action, they do not rule out more limited and tightly focused action."

A huge and proximate diaspora. "The Haitian diaspora in North America is proportionately one of the largest in the world. It provides Haiti with a massive flow of remittances, a reservoir of skills, and a powerful political lobby."

Market opportunity. "Market access and cost of production are not the only factors of importance. Transport to market is also a fundamental consideration. Many fragile states are landlocked and, therefore, face prohibitive transport costs. In contrast, Haiti is on the doorstep of its market."[30]

Collier made an important observation, saying, "Haiti is not hopeless. . . . In view of the above, the air of despondency apparent in the donor community is inappropriate."

Since this optimistic outlook report, Haiti has experienced a

[30] Collier, "Haiti: From Natural Catastrophe to Economic Security."

series of calamities, including:

- two major earthquakes with devastating consequences;
- intractable political unrests in which politicians used the ridiculous
- strategy of violently shutting down the country (peyi lòk) to force out a duly elected president;
- the murder in his residence of a democratically elected and ruling president;
- the eruption of monstrously violent gangs engaging in kidnappings, killings, rapes with impunity under the watch of an apparently indifferent or complacent government;
- a government that has hoisted the white flag of defeat and surrender,
- relying on the sole plan of asking the international community to send military forces to uproot the gangs that officials and oligarchs have created, used, or tolerated.

Why did Haiti descend into the bottomless pit of chaos and despair? The winds of division and instability have significantly reduced the space in the slightly open political window Collier pointed to. No visionary leadership has arisen to take responsibility for the development, even the decent survival of the country. Because everything rises and falls on leadership, rudderless leaders have generated a chaotic society. Beyond an amazing potential and favorable geography, a nation first exists, then prospers, in her leaders' psyche. Also, communities thrive on a clear sense of identity, raison d'être, and supportive collective imagination. In short, they thrive on culture.

Haiti's new beginning can draw inspiration from the legacy of global leaders who exemplified resilience, unity, and transformational change in their nations. Toussaint Louverture, Haiti's own revolutionary hero, led the first successful slave rebellion, proving that a resilient spirit and a united front can overcome seemingly insurmountable odds. Like Gandhi in India, Louverture harnessed a powerful vision of liberation for all, despite the oppressive forces surrounding him. Gandhi's nonviolent methods showed that change could stem from a place of peace rather than conflict, teaching that the power to unite people often lies in shared values and a steadfast dedication to justice. A renewed Haiti could emerge by reawakening Louverture's spirit of solidarity, coupled with Gandhi's lessons of nonviolence, fostering a movement that empowers citizens and ignites a collective hope for peace, equality, and freedom.

Haiti's journey forward can also draw inspiration from the visions of Martin Luther King Jr., Nelson Mandela, and Barack Obama, whose leadership emphasized reconciliation, dignity, and inclusive progress. Intertwined with his spiritual conviction, King's message of equality highlighted the importance of human dignity in achieving social harmony, a principle Haiti must adopt to end divisions and foster a culture of respect. Mandela's triumph over apartheid demonstrated the importance of forgiveness and healing, offering Haiti a roadmap to bridge historical divides and reshape its identity through reconciliation. Obama's rise to the US presidency proved that change is possible even against skepticism and an inconducive climate; his vision of "hope" and "change" resonated worldwide. By building a collective vision inspired by these leaders, Haiti can usher in an era of growth, unity, and resilience rooted in peace, justice, and shared prosperity ideals.

CHAPTER 5
DEVELOPING A CULTURE OF PEACE

It is easier to lead men to combat, stirring up their passion, than to restrain and direct them toward the patient labors of peace.[31] *André Gide, French writer*

Irenology presents peace both as a moral imperative and a practical necessity. This value offers a path to healing and transformation and can be achieved through deliberate effort. It is the foundation upon which societies can build enduring prosperity, stable governance, and vibrant, uplifting cultures. True peace is a form of wealth that surpasses material riches; it enriches the spirit, nurtures human potential, and fosters societal cohesion, leading to integral development.

Although peace remains a daunting goal to achieve in Haiti, where the wounds of the past still run deep, engineering adequate public policies, cultural shifts, and community initiatives will help address the root causes of violence, inequality, and despair that have long plagued our society.

The need to develop a culture of peace has never been more pressing. This journey is neither easy nor straightforward, but it offers immense rewards. Haiti must embed peace at the core of its values and practices to pave the way for a more just, equitable, and harmonious society.

The dividends of peace are not confined to any single domain; they ripple through every aspect of life, from the

[31] Gide and Sheridan, The Immoralist.

economy to social cohesion and political stability. Peace is the foundation for sustainable development, equitable political systems, and cohesive societies. Across the globe, from ancient civilizations to modern nations, the pursuit of peace has been a universal aspiration, a lofty ideal that transcends cultural, political, and geographical boundaries. It is a vision of a world where individuals and communities can thrive, free from the fear of violence and the harrowing constraints of injustice.

I recently visited the Underwater Museum in Mexico, showcasing peace's transcendental value. The Submarine Peace Statues between Cancun and Isla Mujeres are part of an exhibition created in 2009 to combine art and environmental conservation. The installation features more than five hundred life-sized sculptures on the seafloor representing various themes, particularly peace. Renato, the guide, explained that the peace statues symbolize harmony, unity, and the importance of living in balance with the surroundings.

The underwater environment adds another layer of meaning as the statues gradually transform over time, becoming covered with coral and marine life. This natural growth represents the healing power of peace and restoration, illustrating that, like ecosystems, societies need time and collective effort to repair and thrive. The evolving nature of the sculptures serves as a reminder that peace is not a static goal but a continuous process requiring attention and nurturing.

Peace fosters a climate of innovation and creativity. In environments free from the fear of violence and instability, individuals are more likely to take risks, innovate, and contribute to their societies' cultural and intellectual development. Whether through the arts, sciences, or entrepreneurship, peace fosters creative expression and societal progress. Peace also enhances international relationships and global standing. Nations known for their stability and peacefulness are more likely to form positive diplomatic and trade relationships, further strengthening their economies and influence on the world stage.

In many ways, peace is the most valuable asset Haiti can possess. While material wealth often captures attention through natural resources, industrial output, or financial markets, peace creates an environment where such wealth can be generated, sustained, and shared. Like many nations with a turbulent past, Haiti offers a clear example of how the absence of peace can hinder wealth accumulation and equitable distribution. However, the inverse is equally true; when peace is treated as the foundation of national development, it can lead to prosperity far beyond material riches. Without the steadying hand of peace, these opportunities are often left unrealized. True wealth for Haiti does not lie solely in its untapped resources or potential but in its ability to foster a stable, peaceful environment where these resources can be effectively harnessed.

Beyond its economic benefits, peace also nurtures human capital development, which is arguably a nation's greatest asset. In a peaceful society, individuals can pursue education, improve their health, and develop skills without fearing violence or instability. Peace would empower Haiti's young population to contribute to its future by investing in their development. Education systems thrive in peaceful contexts, allowing children to grow up with the knowledge and tools they need to become productive members of society.

Moreover, peace fosters an environment where healthcare can improve, reducing the toll that violence and insecurity take on physical and mental well-being. The result is a healthier, more educated, and more capable workforce, which is the foundation of any prosperous nation.

Peace also contributes to the development of cultural and spiritual wealth, while the absence of peace can stifle cultural expression as people become preoccupied with survival and conflict management. In a peaceful Haiti, cultural life would flourish, with citizens and communities able to express themselves fully and share their heritage with the world. Peace provides the space for creativity, allowing artists, musicians, and thinkers to contribute to the national dialogue and the global cultural landscape. This cultural wealth is invaluable, as it strengthens national identity, fosters unity, and provides a source of pride for future generations.

In addition to fostering economic, human, and cultural wealth, peace in Haiti would lead to a stronger sense of social cohesion. In a peaceful Haiti, communities would be better equipped to work together toward common goals, rebuilding infrastructure, improving public services, or developing local economies. This sense of solidarity is a form of wealth in itself, as it enables societies to be resilient in the face of external challenges and internal pressures.

Building and sustaining peace within a nation requires deliberate, well-thought-out policies that address the root causes of conflict and foster conditions for long-term stability. Peace cannot flourish in a vacuum; it must be supported by systems and structures that promote justice, equity, and opportunity for all citizens. By integrating peace studies into the education system from an early age, Haiti can foster a generation that understands the value of peaceful coexistence and is equipped with the tools to resolve disputes without violence. Countries such as Costa Rica and South Africa, which have implemented peace education programs, offer powerful examples of how such policies can contribute to social cohesion and national healing.

Inclusive governance is another critical component of nurturing peace. Political systems that are open, transparent, and participatory create an environment in which all citizens feel represented and heard. Haiti's political instability has often been driven by exclusionary practices and a lack of trust in government institutions; therefore, policies promoting inclusive governance are essential. This means creating mechanisms for civic participation at the local and national levels, ensuring marginalized groups have a voice in decision-making processes.

Decentralization can foster greater inclusion, empowering communities to take charge of their own development and resolve local issues without relying solely on national authorities. Inclusive governance can reduce tensions, build trust, and create a more stable political environment by giving citizens a stake in their government and the decisions that affect their lives.

Another policy area crucial to peacebuilding is the establishment of strong, independent institutions that uphold the rule of law. Accountable institutions are vital to contain the corruption that has undermined trust in government and weakened democratic processes. Policies aimed at strengthening the judiciary, combating corruption, and ensuring the law is applied fairly to all citizens are necessary for a culture of justice. When people believe they can rely on the legal system to protect their rights and provide recourse in times of conflict, they are less likely to take matters into their own hands. The rule of law provides a foundation for peace by ensuring that disputes are resolved through legitimate, peaceful channels rather than superstition, violence, or retribution.

A culture of peace requires shifts in how societies view justice and accountability. In cultures where retribution is seen as the primary form of justice, cycles of violence often perpetuate. A culture of peace, by contrast, promotes restorative justice that focuses on healing, reconciliation, and making amends rather than punishment. Adopting a restorative approach to justice could be transformative. This approach would involve creating spaces for truth-telling, forgiveness, and healing, allowing communities to move forward from past harms. As a fundamental component of building enduring peace, restorative justice stresses rebuilding social harmony and healing relationships. Community-based justice programs focusing on mediation, dialogue, and reconciliation can help shift the cultural mindset from revenge to restoration.

Further, peace must be nurtured through policies that promote social dialogue and reconciliation. Promoting reconciliation between different groups is essential for healing and building unity. National reconciliation programs that bring together political, social, and community leaders to engage in dialogue can help bridge divides and address historical grievances.

A culture of peace in Haiti requires building solidarity across different social and economic groups. Solidarity is the recognition that all members of a society are linked and that one's own welfare depends on the welfare of all. This sense of shared responsibility is vital for fostering peace, as it encourages people to work together toward common goals rather than viewing each other as competitors or adversaries. Fostering solidarity could involve initiatives that bring together different communities to address shared challenges, such as poverty, unemployment, or environmental degradation. These joint efforts build practical solutions and strengthen social bonds, creating a sense of collective ownership over the future.

Developing a culture of peace requires intentional cultural shifts that promote empathy, nonviolent conflict resolution, and solidarity. For Haiti, these shifts are necessary for resolving current conflicts and preventing future ones. By promoting a national narrative of unity, normalizing peaceful conflict resolution, and building empathy and solidarity across divides, Haiti can embrace a culture where peace is not only possible but deeply ingrained in the values and practices of its people. As these cultural shifts take root, they will reinforce the policies and structures that support peace, creating a stable and harmonious society for generations to come.

The global ideal of peace has become increasingly pressing. Nations recognize that peace is a collective endeavor that requires cooperation, dialogue, and sustained effort from all corners of the world. International frameworks and agreements have long been established to promote global peace. Institutions such as the

United Nations (UN) and its peacekeeping missions, along with organizations like the Organization of American States (OAS), the International Criminal Court (ICC), the World Trade Organization (WTO), and the Caribbean Community (CARICOM) are all rooted in the idea that global peace is achievable through collaboration and the rule of law. The UN's Sustainable Development Goals (SDGs), particularly Goal 16, emphasize peace, justice, and strong institutions as key to global prosperity.

Initiatives such as these have helped reduce conflict and promote stability in many regions worldwide, offering frameworks for nations to address the underlying causes of violence and instability. Through these mechanisms, the global quest for peace has become an institutionalized effort, reflecting the belief that the future of humanity is intrinsically tied to the peaceful coexistence of all nations.

Despite its internal challenges, Haiti has a unique potential to contribute to the global peace movement. History confers on Haiti a special role in conversations about justice and freedom. Haiti's revolutionary past symbolizes the fight against oppression, but its ongoing struggle for stability and peace reflects the complexities many nations face today. Haiti's potential contribution to global peace lies in its ability to transform its history of struggle into one of resilience and hope. Haiti can offer valuable lessons to the world about the importance of reconciliation, forgiveness, and national unity.

To play its role fully on the international scene and contribute to peace worldwide, Haiti must address the roots of enduring and widespread violence. Systemic problems and entrenched practices severely affect the majority of the population and perpetuate a cycle of violence.

One of the most harmful practices is nepotism and political favoritism in public sector employment. Jobs and opportunities are often distributed based on political connections rather than merit, creating widespread exclusion and resentment. This practice leaves qualified citizens, especially those from rural and marginalized communities, without pathways to meaningful employment. The resulting socioeconomic divides deepen frustration and foster a sense of disenfranchisement, prompting protests and civil disobedience. These expressions of dissent are often met with violent crackdowns, reinforcing the cycle of violence.

Corruption and the misallocation of public funds further exacerbate these issues. When resources that should be directed toward essential services are funneled into inflated salaries for high-ranking officials or an inefficient security apparatus, the public's basic needs remain unmet. This leads to widespread poverty and hopelessness, which frequently spill over into violent demonstrations. Instead of addressing underlying inequalities, the government's reliance on security forces to maintain control only deepens the instability.

A glaring example of inequality is seen in public sector salaries. While teachers and healthcare workers earn as little as $150 per month, often facing delayed payments, members of parliament and senior officials can receive more than ten thousand dollars monthly, along with substantial benefits. This stark imbalance illustrates the disconnect between the governing elite and regular civil servants, contributing to resentment.

Despite being under-administered, Haiti continues to create high-paying, politically motivated positions while essential services are neglected, especially in rural areas. This prioritization reflects a governance model marked by social exclusion and elitism, which inflicts psychological violence on the wider population. This exclusion becomes palpable when skilled Haitians, unable to find work in their home country, are forced to migrate for low-paying jobs abroad.

Statistics further illustrate these inequities:

Teacher-to-Student Ratio: Pupil-teacher ratio, primary in Haiti was 33.41 as of 1998. Its highest value over the past 27 years was 52.36 in 1972, while its lowest value was 30.88 in 1993, compared to the global average of 24:1 (UNESCO)[32].

Healthcare Workers: Haiti has approximately one doctor per ten thousand people and one nurse per five thousand, far below the World Health Organization's recommendation of twenty-three healthcare workers per 10,000 people.[33]

Public Administration: The country has fewer than eight public sector workers per one thousand inhabitants[34], whereas the Latin American has a range between 19 and 53

Corruption Perception: Haiti ranks 172 out of 180 countries on Transparency International's Corruption Perception Index[35].

These figures highlight the severe disparities in public service compensation and staffing. Nepotism, political patronage, and geographical discrimination further restrict access to public sector jobs for the majority of Haitians. The result is a cycle where inadequate services, low wages, and corruption disenfranchise the population, fueling periodic violent uprisings.

Haiti maintains fifty-three embassies and consulates worldwide, staffed by numerous diplomats and overseas agents representing the country abroad. While this network aims to foster international relations, it contrasts starkly with the government's minimal presence in rural regions, where most Haitians live. In these rural areas, essential governance structures and public services are often absent or severely under-resourced, leaving communities without access to basic necessities like healthcare, education, and justice. This imbalance underscores a system prioritizing external representation over internal development, exacerbating feelings of neglect and exclusion.

The disparity between the extensive diplomatic network and the limited government presence in rural Haiti highlights a

---

[32] "Education for All in Haiti over the Last 20 Years: Assessment and Perspectives - UNESCO Digital Library."

[33] Gallagher et al., "Pan American Health Organization/World Health Organization Collaborating Centers in Nursing and Midwifery in Haiti."

[34] "Rfph_201802.Pdf."

[35] "Haiti - Transparency.Org."

profound misalignment in national priorities. Equitable governance must reach all corners of the country for true peace and nation-building. The overinvestment in overseas diplomatic representation, contrasted with the underfunding of rural infrastructure and services, reflects an elitist governance approach and hinders efforts to create unity, trust, and stability within the nation.

The judicial system is another major contributor to chronic violence. Widespread corruption, inefficiency, and dysfunction result in prolonged pretrial detention and a lack of access to justice. More than 80 percent of the prison population in Haiti is in pretrial detention[36], trapped in overcrowded and unsanitary conditions, exacerbating frustration and anger. The absence of fair legal recourse alienates large swaths of the population, fostering distrust and pushing people toward mob justice and violent retribution.

Barriers to entrepreneurship and economic participation further compound the problem. Without access to credit and with bureaucratic and corrupt business licensing practices, many Haitians are prevented from starting or expanding businesses. This forces enterprising individuals into the informal economy, limiting economic empowerment and entrenching poverty, especially in rural and marginalized urban areas.

These challenges fuel a cycle of violence, as those who feel excluded and powerless turn to uprisings as their only recourse, eroding trust in institutions and perpetuating instability.

The legacy of exclusion, including historic injustices surrounding land ownership, deepens the cycle of poverty and underfunded public services. Jean-Jacques Dessalines, the leader of Haiti's independence, once asked, "And the Blacks, whose fathers are in Africa, will they not have anything?" This question remains relevant today.

Comprehensive reform is essential to break this cycle and

[36] "Haiti - United States Department of State."

create an equitable, inclusive public sector. Such reform is the pathway to lasting peace, as peace thrives where individuals can reach their potential, have their rights protected, and feel their voices are heard.

The road to peace is long and often fraught with difficulties, but it is worth traveling. Peace is not only an end goal but an ongoing process that requires the collective efforts of government, civil society, local communities, and individuals. By nurturing peace as a form of wealth, Haiti can lay the groundwork for a future where all its people can thrive. Peace offers the opportunity to build a nation where justice prevails, opportunities abound, and community bonds are strengthened.

CHAPTER 6

EMBRACING FORGIVENESS AND RECONCILIATION

See that no one pays back evil for evil to anyone, but always pursue what is good for one another and for all. 1 Thes 5: 15

Grudges are drinking poison in the hope that the other person will die. Nelson Mandela, Former President of South Africa

The recent disturbing years in the life of the Haitian people beg the question of their desire to live together as a nation and to chart a collective uplifting destiny. Threats of all kinds weigh on the survival of peaceful citizens and their chances of progress. The foundation of society has suffered severe cracks as many leaders become ringleaders or turncoats and betray their oath of office. Non-state criminal groupings challenge the government and bring terror to citizens with impunity. Destruction of life and property degrades the country to a patch of wilderness and shadow of death.

A military or police solution would be inadequate. In Petite Riviere de l'Artibonite, my hometown, more than two hundred heavily armed gang members with trucks and motorcycles attacked the population, going from home to home, stealing, killing, raping, and destroying property. The city police station was abandoned even before the attack, and no police officer was in view to heed the cries of the victims. In many other areas, similar situations happened. Now, how many of these numerous gang members should be killed for peace to prevail? Even after destroying them, how will society prevent the rise of other mass criminals?

The chaos and anarchy in Haiti are of political and socio-economic origin. It doesn't submit to the use of force alone, especially when political and law enforcement officers are in cahoots with criminals.

Further, law enforcement officers wielding legitimate violence on behalf of the state cannot use lex talionis (the law of retaliation) or the same methods as the gangs. They operate on lofty principles of respect for life, decency, and protection of private property. The goal of law enforcement officers is not to destroy individuals engaged in banditry but to preserve peace by destroying banditry. In the end, society wants criminals to face punishment or restoration as law-abiding citizens.

God declares: *"Vengeance is mine, retribution is mine" (Rom 12: 19)*. Self-defense groups' attempts to do justice to themselves can only deepen social divisions and darken our prospects for socio-economic development. Applying mob expeditious justice and administering whimsical execution by stoning or immolation is tantamount to adding cruelty to cruelty and atrocity to atrocity. Fire is put out with water, not with more fire. Love, not perpetuating a cycle of violence, is the key to ending hate and conflict.

The only solution to Haiti's protean and never-ending crisis is to engage our compatriots in loving one another for their own sake and the sake of the nation. As Martin Luther King Jr. said: *"We must learn to live together as brothers; otherwise we will all die together like idiots."*

A holistic approach must prevail because the situation is so delicate and complex. Cool heads and wisdom must prevail on behalf of Haitians' common humanity. If we are to plug the cracks of society's shaky foundation, we must show the courage to embrace forgiveness and reconciliation for lasting peace. Restorative justice must be a powerful arrow in our quiver.

And every Haitian can and must play their part, as they are called to forgive their offenders and to reconcile with them. Everyone can play a role in their circle of influence, although major national decisions, trust between political actors, and public policies to bring peace, security, and order may be beyond the grasp of regular citizens. Each Haitian can contribute forgiveness and reconciliation for peace and the advancement of their community and country.

Societies worldwide are realizing the power of forgiveness and reconciliation to bring peace and create conditions for a lasting commitment to progress.

On November 19, 2019, during a meeting of the UN Security Council on the role of reconciliation in the maintenance of international peace and security, Secretary-General António Guterres said:

> *Successful reconciliation helps prevent the resurgence of conflict, in addition to forming the breeding ground for more resilient societies, peaceful and prosperous. This is especially true in the wake of large-scale violence and human rights violations. . . . From Cambodia to Rwanda, via Northern Ireland and Bosnia and Herzegovina, reconciliation processes helped to resolve ethnic, religious, and political conflicts. . . . It is for this reason that promoting reconciliation and breaking the cycle of impunity is an integral part of our work. . . .*
>
> *Reconciliation must come from within, with the participation of all, including women, civil society, religious leaders and youth. . . . Reconciliation cannot be a substitute for justice, or even open the way to amnesty for the most serious crimes.*[37]

Regarding forgiveness, the philosopher Jacques Derrida

[37] "Reconciliation Must Evolve to Reflect Growing Complexity of Today's Conflicts, Participants Stress during Day-Long Security Council Open Debate | Meetings Coverage and Press Releases."

explains: *"Today scenes of forgiveness are multiplying on the face of the earth. Heads of state are asking forgiveness from a population or other states in Europe and throughout the world. . . . This generalization means that the religious, let's say biblical, Judeo-Christian and Islamic value of forgiveness is in the process of marking the entire geopolitical space, beyond the strict state authorities."*[38]

Author Candice Mama, whose father, Glenack Masilo Mama, was tortured and burned alive by the Afrikaner police colonel Eugene de Kock during the apartheid era in South Africa, wrote: *"I couldn't hate de Kock, because love and hate can't operate in the same space. If I wanted to hold a grudge against him, I could never fully enjoy the life for which my father and so many others died, voluntarily or not. He had stolen a father from me, and I had unconsciously offered him 16 years of anger, anguish, sleepless nights, bouts of deep depression, continuous thoughts, and suicide attempts. One day, I simply refused to let him continue to take away my enthusiasm and zest for life. So, I did what I had to do, I forgave him."*[39]

Despite its centuries-old heartbreaking trials and tribulations, Haiti still struggles to integrate forgiveness and reconciliation into its culture. The government initiative closest to this concept was the establishment of the National Commission for Truth and Justice (CNVJ) in 1995. Such a commission has also functioned in countries such as South Africa, Chile, Ecuador, Guatemala, Liberia, Morocco, Nigeria, Peru, El Salvador, Sierra Leone, Sri Lanka, Timor-Leste, and Uruguay.

The Governance and Social Development Resource Centre (GSDRC) commented on the results of the CNVJ: "The Commission faced many complications (including a lack of political will and funding) and numerous institutional constraints (including lack of capacity, increasing security concerns, and shortages of time and funding). The Commission was, therefore, unable to contribute appropriately to the acknowledgment of Haiti's conflicted past, undermining donor attempts to advance

[38] Derrida, On Cosmopolitanism and Forgiveness.
[39] "How I Forgave the Man Who Murdered My Father | British Council."

reconciliation in the country."[40]

Apart from the attempt of the CNVJ, civil society organizations occasionally called for forgiveness and reconciliation. For example, in April 2022, Pastor Calixte Fleuridor, president of the Protestant Federation of Haiti (FPH), launched a call for reconciliation and forgiveness to all sectors of Haiti. The Episcopal Conference of Haiti (CEH) sent letters to men and women of goodwill in favor of forgiveness and reconciliation.

These contributions are necessary but not sufficient. A systematic approach and an ongoing commitment are prerequisites to bottom-up cultural change. Churches, prayer groups, civil society organizations, the media, and government institutions should join forces to further the advent of forgiveness and reconciliation. Every man and every woman in Haiti must seek to cultivate a loving, compassionate, and caring heart—a heart that forgives and seeks reconciliation.

Forgiveness is the conscious, deliberate decision to release feelings of resentment or vengeance toward a person or group who has harmed you, regardless of whether they deserve your forgiveness. It is not about forgetting or excusing the harm done, but rather, it is about freeing yourself from the burden of anger and hatred. In the context of Haiti, forgiveness is a critical step toward healing the deep-seated wounds caused by historical and ongoing conflicts. It is a powerful tool that can transform relationships, rebuild trust, and pave the way for genuine reconciliation.

The act of forgiveness has profound psychological and emotional benefits. Presumably, forgiving others can lead to lower levels of stress and anxiety, improved mental health, and greater overall well-being. When individuals let go of grudges and bitterness, they often experience a sense of relief and inner peace.

[40] "Haiti's Failed Truth Commission: Lessons in Transitional Justice - GSDRC."

For communities, forgiveness can reduce collective tensions and promote a more harmonious social environment. In Haiti, where many people have experienced trauma and loss, forgiveness can help individuals and communities move forward from past hurts and build a more resilient and supportive society.

Throughout history, numerous examples of forgiveness have led to powerful transformations in societies. One such instance is South Africa following post-apartheid, where the Truth and Reconciliation Commission (TRC) was instrumental in correcting past injustices. The TRC created a forum for offenders and victims to tell their stories and ask for and receive pardon, thus promoting healing and peace in the country.

Another example is the Rwandan Gacaca courts, which were established to address the aftermath of the 1994 genocide. These community-based courts facilitated restorative justice and reconciliation, allowing survivors and perpetrators to coexist and rebuild their communities. These examples highlight the potential of forgiveness to heal divisions and create a foundation for lasting peace.

Creating awareness about the importance of forgiveness is the first step in fostering a culture of reconciliation. This involves educating the public about the benefits of forgiveness and its role in personal and societal healing. Awareness campaigns can take various forms, including workshops, seminars, and media campaigns highlighting stories of forgiveness and reconciliation. Schools can integrate lessons on forgiveness into their curricula, teaching children the value of empathy and understanding from a young age. By raising awareness, we can begin to shift societal attitudes toward a more forgiving and compassionate mindset.

Open and honest dialogue is crucial for fostering forgiveness. Creating spaces where individuals and groups can share their experiences, grievances, and perspectives without fear of judgment or retribution is essential. These dialogues can take place in various settings, such as community meetings, town halls, or through organized peace-building initiatives. Facilitators trained in conflict resolution can help guide these conversations, ensuring they remain constructive and focused on healing. Constructive dialogue helps to break down barriers, build mutual understanding, and pave the way for reconciliation.

Truth and Reconciliation Commissions (TRCs) are formal, structured bodies that uncover and address past injustices and human rights violations. They are essential in reconciliation because they give victims a stage to tell their stories and allow offenders to own their actions. These commissions focus on uncovering the truth, fostering understanding, and promoting healing. In Haiti, a TRC could help address historical grievances and current conflicts by creating a comprehensive record of past abuses, facilitating a national dialogue on justice, and recommending measures to prevent future atrocities. The transparency and inclusivity of TRCs can help build trust in public institutions and lay the groundwork for a more just and peaceful society.

While formal structures like TRCs are essential, grassroots efforts and community-based programs are equally vital in fostering reconciliation. These initiatives focus on healing at the local level, where the impacts of conflict are often most deeply felt. Community-based approaches can include peace circles, restorative justice programs, and local mediation efforts. These initiatives bring together community members to address conflicts, share stories, and find common ground.

Community leaders, including religious figures, can be crucial in guiding these processes and ensuring they resonate with local values and experiences. These leaders can use their platforms to preach the message of forgiveness, understanding, and unity. By organizing interfaith dialogues and community events, they can bring together diverse groups and promote a culture of peace.

Cultural and social barriers can significantly hinder efforts toward forgiveness and reconciliation in Haiti. Traditional beliefs and practices, while rich and diverse, sometimes emphasize retribution over reconciliation. Long-standing prejudices and mistrust between different groups can also create significant obstacles. These cultural norms can make it difficult for individuals to embrace forgiveness, as it may be perceived as a sign of weakness or betrayal of their group's suffering. Furthermore, the concerns of oppressed groups may fall on deaf ears due to how social hierarchies and power dynamics maintain and even amplify existing causes of conflict.

Attempts at forgiveness and reconciliation may encounter opposition from various sources. People and organizations who have experienced severe trauma may not choose to let go of their hurt and rage. The current strife and division may also serve political and economic interests. Therefore, the solution to this resistance calls for a diversified strategy. To those who have suffered from serious violence and loss, psychological support and trauma recovery are crucial. Thus, the militants of reconciliation must highlight concrete advantages, such as increased security, better community cohesiveness, and economic opportunity, to promote broader acceptance.

Political and law enforcement leaders must understand the motivations, linkages, and structures of gangs and bandits to tackle the core causes of anarchy and develop effective remedies. Criminal organizations often emerge from complicated social, economic, and political factors, including poverty, unemployment, social exclusion, and a lack of reliable state institutions. In addition to financial benefits, gang membership can give individuals a sense of belonging, safety, and authority in a chaotic environment. By examining the underlying issues, authorities may develop measures that address the motives of gang membership and provide alternatives for young people and underprivileged populations who are typically dragged into the cycle of violence.

Eliminating gangs and bandits' power structures requires an awareness of individual motivations and a comprehension of their relationships with other components of society. These ties frequently include unscrupulous politicians, dishonest public servants, corrupt law enforcement officers, corporations, and global networks providing arms or laundering funds. Without tackling these interconnected linkages, anti-crime initiatives will likely be short-lived and unsustainable. Detailed mapping of these networks enables more focused actions, like severing funding sources, bringing charges against complicit officials, and putting in place neighborhood initiatives that upend the social networks that support gang activity.

Moreover, addressing gang violence requires an awareness of the systems in which these groups operate, including the informal economies, territorial control, and community dynamics that sustain them. Gangs in Haiti often fill the vacuum left by a weak state, providing their own forms of "governance" or social order in areas where government services are absent. Plans must include social development programs that enhance the population's quality of life while bolstering the presence of state institutions to counteract the vacuum of legitimate authorities. The government can weaken the structures that support criminal activity and lessen the allure of gang life while promoting long-term peace and stability by substituting lawful services and opportunities for the roles that gangs provide.

Given Haiti's current severe and unsustainable security, forgiveness and reconciliation are crucial to the country's healing and development. Communities are at risk of violence, extortion, and displacement because law enforcement has not established the capacity to destroy the formidable gangs that control many neighborhoods. Gang strength is not the only factor contributing to their growth; security services' incapacity to properly combat them is another. Addressing the underlying causes of conflict, mending neglected societal scars, and bringing people together via forgiveness and reconciliation are all necessary to end this cycle of violence. This strategy can promote a shared dedication to peace that buttresses the capabilities of any law enforcement organization, facilitating societal reconstruction and healing.

Another example of the pressing need for reconciliation is the abandonment of many police stations. In several areas, there is very no law enforcement presence due to the empty stations, leaving entire towns defenseless and unprotected. Efforts at forgiveness and reconciliation can be very important in rebuilding public confidence in law enforcement. Haiti can progressively rebuild its policing system based on mutual respect by addressing historical grievances and seeking restorative justice. This process would also encourage former gang members and other disaffected youth to reintegrate into society, contributing to a safer and more cohesive community.

Haiti's justice system is in disarray, with damaged or destroyed courthouses and jails and a judiciary that struggles to function. The public has lost faith in legal institutions as a result of the justice system's dysfunction, which also contributes to a culture of impunity, where crimes frequently go unpunished.

A concentrated effort toward reconciliation is required to win back people's trust in the judiciary, which should work to rebuild communities, mend relationships, and enforce the law. This approach can be more effective than traditional punitive measures, fostering a sense of collective healing and societal reintegration vital for the nation's stability.

Moreover, there is a notable absence of a clear security plan in Haiti, along with inadequate equipment and outdated technology. A well-coordinated approach will sustain any long-term advancement in security and peace. Forgiveness and reconciliation can bridge the gap created by institutional failures in a fractured setting. These initiatives can support the development of a common future vision that puts unity above division and peace above retaliation. The foundation for a new, all-encompassing security framework may naturally form as communities unite to forgive past wrongdoings and work out their differences.

Restoring order in Haiti requires an efficient administrative system. Even when available resources are frequently mismanaged or do not reach individuals in need due to a lack of pertinent technology and inefficient administrative procedures. Creating a more effective and open administrative system will foster a culture of forgiveness and integrity. Reform implementation, institutional modernization, and efficient resource use all depend on the collaborative attitude that reconciliation promotes. We can gradually restore the institutional capability required to uphold peace and promote economic growth by working together.

Last but not least, Haiti's profound social differences have fueled a vicious cycle of political instability, violence, and mistrust. Without a concerted effort to bridge these gaps, the nation risks further decline. By urging people to own up to past wrongs and cooperate toward a common goal for Haiti's future, forgiveness and reconciliation can serve as effective means of mending these divisions. This procedure can assist in removing the mental and emotional obstacles that have prevented the country from advancing. Thus, Haiti will move past its tumultuous history and create a more peaceful and wealthy nation where compatriots unite and understand one another.

Every Haitian, whether living in the country or abroad, is responsible for promoting peace and forgiveness. We must acknowledge that forgiveness is a strong act of courage and strength that opens the door to reconciliation and healing rather than a show of weakness.

Maintaining optimism and faith in the potential for a united and peaceful Haiti is crucial. Global narratives of forgiveness and reconciliation serve as a reminder that despite enduring animosities and historical scars, change is achievable. A culture of forgiveness can help transform our communities, heal our nation, and build a future where every Haitian can thrive.

CHAPTER 7

THE RIGHT BRAND OF LEADERSHIP FOR HAITI

Everything rises and falls on leadership. John Maxwell, writer and leadership expert.

Haiti's present turmoil is not a sudden affliction but the product of leadership that has repeatedly prioritized self-preservation over public good. To break free from this cycle, Haiti requires a new brand of leadership that is transformative, principled, and dedicated to the service of its people.

After Haiti gained independence, the descendants of slave owners reclaimed their ancestral properties. Political elites secured their positions by sharing power and resources, leaving most of the population destitute. Because of this division, the marginalized—those without property or education—could not find a way out of the restrictive glass ceiling. Political leaders who seek power through disorder have frequently used the ensuing resentment to fuel violent uprisings and waves of civil unrest.

The United Nations High Commissioner for Human Rights, Volker Türk, painted a dire picture on November 3, 2022: *"Amid continuing gang warfare and a vacuum of law and order, Haiti is on the verge of an abyss."*[41] His depiction included a stark reality of firearm violence, the lack of basic necessities, and rampant impunity for sexual violence. He underlined that immediate action addressing

[41] "Haiti 'on the Verge of an Abyss', Warns UN Rights Chief | UN News."

the fundamental causes of these crises is essential for a long-term recovery. Decades of corruption and the breakdown of the rule of law have ruined the country.

For a long time, Haitian politicians have echoed their people's hopelessness by lamenting the very circumstances their attitude or policies either caused or maintained. They face crises unprepared, waiting for divine intervention or international aid, and lacking vision and accountability. Many leaders have stayed in power by sponsoring armed groups and rewarding allegiance with undue favors rather than building resilience through robust institutions. This cycle of compulsion and neglect has created the conditions for the descent into the abyss.

The issue of governance and leadership in Haiti often evokes a *"dialogue in the underworld between Machiavelli and Montesquieu"*[42], oscillating between realpolitik or a drive for total control and a layback or do-nothing approach, believing that time will heal all the woes.

Haiti must prioritize well-structured, principled leadership if it is to regain a functioning society. As history has demonstrated, nations prosper under the guidance of leaders who protect justice, stoke courage, and inspire trust. Servant and transformational leaders are essential because they foster a sense of belonging to the community and put the good of the group ahead of individual whims and interests.

The attitude that led to Haiti's independence starkly contrasts its current predicament. Generals and the oppressed alike had an unwavering yearning for freedom and dignity, which led to the revolution's victory. That group's determination helped them defeat the most powerful military of their era. The same determination that fueled Haiti's founding can inspire a rebirth today. History teaches us that lasting change comes from leaders with a clear vision and a strong commitment to helping others.

Reversing Haiti's decline begins with developing capable

[42] Bluwal and Joly, Dialogue aux enfers entre Machiavel et Montesquieu.

leaders who can inspire hope and guide the nation with integrity. According to John Maxwell's "Law of the Lid," effective leadership determines an organization's success. Leaders who undermine new ideas and silence competitors hinder progress. This mindset exemplifies the "law of the lid."

Haiti needs servant leaders who prioritize constant learning, self-improvement, and selfless service to others. Toussaint Louverture's example is instructive. Rising from slavery, he transformed himself into an intellectual force, studying the works of philosophers and mastering the art of leadership. Louverture's journey from "Fatras Baton," a sickly youth, to a formidable military strategist underscores the power of personal development driven by love for one's people and the greater good.

Love for God, oneself, and the community must be the cornerstones of this leadership. According to 1 Corinthians 13, this kind of love enables leaders to face difficulties head-on, promote harmony, and behave with integrity. Love-based and service-oriented leaders may lead Haiti toward peace and development by overcoming superstition, ignorance, neglect, and self-indulgence.

Haiti must set up structures that support leadership at all levels to produce such leaders. This policy necessitates integrating ongoing leadership development into civil services, education, and public administration. Teachers, police officers, and other professionals must regularly get training to reinforce the concepts of servant leadership, and elected officials should make a commitment to continuous leadership development.

The history of world leadership demonstrates the revolutionary power of committed people under the aegis of strong institutions. Imagine Singapore without Lee Kuan Yew or the United States without Abraham Lincoln and George Washington. These leaders came from institutions that fostered a sense of duty and service; they did not flourish in isolation.

Relying solely on chance or nature to produce

transformational leaders capable of elevating Haiti is akin to waiting for manna from heaven. For Haiti's renaissance to materialize, its citizens must intentionally nurture the right type of leadership and champion its spread throughout society. Overcoming unfavorable cultural effects will require conscious and continuous efforts.

Haitian leaders who practice positive thinking, constructive communication, and responsible behavior can promote and safeguard the public good, leading to broad improvement. Motivational speaker Jim Rohn aptly stated, "All good will be attacked. Every garden will be invaded; not to think so is naïve. . . . All values must be defended: social values, political values, friendship values, marriage values, family values, and business values. Every garden must be tended all summer. If you don't develop this skill, you'll never wind up with anything of value."

A prevailing belief in Haiti is that the international community will somehow step in to govern indirectly and modernize the country. Historical evidence has shown that such reliance is wishful thinking. Through MINUSTAH and numerous other missions totaling billions of dollars, the United Nations sought to stabilize Haiti and strengthen its political system.

The results? Minimal positive impact, overshadowed by abuse, waste, and a cholera outbreak. The message is clear: Haitians must take control of their development, or progress will be illusive. Foreign leaders will not come to organize political parties, reform public administration, or establish a sustainable economic system. Haiti's cultural revolution and future vision require internal leadership. Haitians are uniquely positioned to accept lifelong learning, wisdom, and self-improvement for the transformation of their country.

Haiti's development requires a political structure that encourages competent leadership and promotes nonviolence, mutual respect, and knowledge, particularly universal literacy. Haiti will secure and enhance its assets when its people break free from their addiction to conflict and violence. The scorched-earth mentality and radicalism that emerge during political crises must end. Establishing and maintaining systems and infrastructure requires years of dedication and substantial resources. A new Haitian mindset will value preservation over destruction.

Haiti has tried several times during its history to overhaul its political structure. In 2014, International IDEA released a book titled Political Parties in the Construction of Democracy in Haiti (Les partis politiques dans la construction de la démocratie en Haïti[43]), under the direction of Laënnec Hurbon, with contributions from Alain Gilles and Franklin Midy. They noted that Haiti's political landscape saw two significant periods of party development: from 1870 to 1883 and 1915 to 1956.

The first period saw the emergence of the Liberal Party and the National Party, neither of which had strong societal roots. While the National Party, with its journal Le Peuple, argued for "power to the greater number, focusing on equality and participation," the Liberal Party published the weekly Le Civilisateur promoting "power to the most capable." The conflict between these parties, predominantly in Port-au-Prince and a few provincial towns, culminated in violent power struggles that ultimately led to their mutual demise.

The second period, from 1915 to 1957, began with the American occupation. During this time, the Patriotic Union brought together various factions and led urban protests against the occupiers. One of its founders, Sténio Vincent, later assumed power and banned the Union to stifle opposition. Following the occupation, two new parties emerged: the Haitian Communist Party (PCH) and the Popular Socialist Party (PSP). Both were critical of racial and colorist rhetoric employed in previous political discourse.

Following the fall of the Duvalier regime in 1986, Haiti saw a plethoric increase in political party creation, from 121 parties

[43] "Les-Partis-Politiques-Dans-La-Construction-Haiti.Pdf."

recognized by the Ministry of Justice in 2014 to 229 in 2023. Yet, despite the proliferation of parties, destructive cultural and politicalemb habits persisted, including the use of force and an adherence to the "end justifies the means" philosophy. Many political groups resorted to violence, directly or through militias, to seize and maintain power. This pattern continued under President Jovenel Moïse, whose tenure saw violent protests instigated by the opposition "Democratic and Popular Sector," causing nationwide disruption.

From the "Tonton Macoute" under Duvalier to the "Chimè" during Aristide's leadership and the gang affiliations during Michel Martelly's administration, the reliance on violence and intimidation has stained Haiti's political landscape. This culture of fear and power manipulation must end. Consequentialism, the belief that the end justifies the means, has only led to societal breakdown. Haitians must champion and defend a culture rooted in nonviolence and love to pave the way for peace and development.

Jean Price-Mars, the Haitian philosopher and diplomat, captured the duality of Haitian culture: *"We could very rightly define the Haitian: a people who sing and who suffer, who struggle and who laugh, a people who laugh, who dance and resign themselves. From birth to death, the song is associated with his whole life."*[44] This remark reflects a culture marked by suffering, a relentless pursuit of pleasure, and resignation. Such traits have slowed progress, creating complacency with poverty, illiteracy, and violence.

However, this culture is not an irreversible fate but a choice—albeit an unconscious one. It can be transformed through visionary leadership and sustained public education. A top priority must be to shift Haiti's culture toward one that values knowledge, hard work, and social harmony. Toussaint Louverture's life offers a model for this transformation. His relentless pursuit of personal growth and dedication to his people demonstrate that determined action makes cultural change possible.

[44] Price-Mars and Shannon, So Spoke the Uncle.

Haiti does not suffer from a lack of intellectual talent but rather from a deficiency in moral resolve. To make progress, we need to love the people around us, believe in their abilities and have hope for a better future. Leaders with these qualities will be honest, fair, and steadfast in pursuing justice without favoritism.

Visionary and servant leadership are based on love, faith, and hope. They bring about changes in culture and speed up growth. History is full of examples of great leaders who lived by these ideals and used them to guide their actions.

It would be unrealistic to think everyone will automatically embrace love, faith, and hope. Just as bad forces grow with the help of people, good change needs passionate supporters who live by these virtues every day. Leaders and influential people in Haiti need to ensure that love, faith, and hope are a part of all of their policies, laws, official procedures, and public conversations. Then, the country can move on from its experience of fear and division and look forward to a future of unity, progress, and hope.

This committed and widespread cultural shift is the only way to break Haiti's cycle of destruction and rebuild a nation poised for progress and prosperity.

The political leaders must be the heralds and torchbearers of this new way of living. Instead of second-guessing and being afraid of their fellow contestants, they must harbor and show confidence in the goodwill and intention of everyone. They will spread forgiveness and reconciliation instead of refusing to shake hands with their adversaries. Instead of refusing to sit at the same table with their opponents, they will promote dialogue and fraternity. Instead of requiring foreigners to mediate between them, they will fully grasp their identity as children in the same family and be responsible for working together in the same motherland's interest. Such an attitude will indeed express the exaltation of our common humanity and mark a new beginning for Haiti.

A reformed political system promotes the rule of law and

prevents anarchy and authoritarianism. It should be simple for citizens to comprehend and use while also ensuring stability through checks and balances.

Experience indicates that a two- or three-party system can promote governance stability. Models like Westminster and presidential systems have proven effective in many countries when supported by the right philosophies and respect for institutions.

Haiti's past struggles with multi-party systems highlight the dangers of a fragmented political landscape driven by leaders' unchecked ambition. However, both the Westminster and presidential systems can foster stability. The regional example of CARICOM provides Haiti with a framework of successful governance and political stability. Similarly, the Dominican Republic's mitigation of political fragmentation through its dominant parties offers valuable insights.

While serving as OAS Representative in Antigua and Barbuda, I witnessed the Westminster system at work. Despite heated political debates, leaders maintained civility. The opposition was present at major national events and shadowed government ministers to promote accountability and informed governance. This approach demonstrates how good leadership, respect for processes, and a functioning legal system promote stability.

In Guyana, where I spent more than six years promoting various cooperative projects, the Westminster-style system was critical in maintaining stability among social and political diversity. The proportional representation system ensured representation across the country's ethnic groups despite tensions fueled by historical election rigging and resource distribution disparities.

The 2020 election, labeled the "mother of all elections" due to the stakes surrounding newly discovered oil wealth, tested the system. Adherence to legal procedures and the presence of international observers maintained electoral integrity and avoided a spiral into chaos. Guyana has resisted the temptation to descend into disorder and turmoil thanks to the Westminster-style system, which includes two powerful and well-established political parties, a functional court, and international support.

Widespread education and adherence to the law are two further elements that contribute to the Westminster system's success in the Caribbean. At first, nations like Ghana and Kenya followed the Westminster model, but they encountered difficulties that caused them to switch to presidential systems. These changes highlight the need for political structures to adjust to the socioeconomic conditions of their environments.

Presidential regimes have promoted stability throughout Latin America by clearly separating the government branches. Scholar José Antonio Cheibub points out that the resilience of these systems often depends on the context of their establishment, particularly in countries transitioning from military rule. Regardless of the system, success hinges on its alignment with societal values and the competence of leaders[45].

Both parliamentarian and presidential systems, or variations thereof, work in many countries. Either system can sustain stability and growth. Haiti usually favors a strong presidential system. However, the country has not been able to maintain stability. Democracy takes root and flourishes when the population has reached a state of receptivity with the ability to grasp, commit to, and participate in the political processes. This determining factor prevents downward slides into dysfunctional levels.

Also, financing political parties and electoral campaigns is paramount to the smooth running of democracy. In 2014, the International Institute for Democracy and Electoral Assistance published a handbook on political finance titled Funding of Political Parties and Election Campaigns.

In his foreword to the handbook, former UN Secretary-General Kofi Annan wrote:

"Over the course of my career, I have witnessed the negative impact of money on politics and governance. There is increasing evidence that

[45] Cheibub, Presidentialism, Parliamentarism, and Democracy.

corruption and unregulated donations are exercising undue influence on politics and undermining the integrity of elections. In some countries, money from organized crime has infiltrated politics to gain control over elected officials and public institutions. These threats to democratic politics help explain why large numbers of people around the world are losing faith in politicians and democratic processes."

Annan added: "In Latin America, West Africa, and many other parts of the world, opaque electoral finance and lack of transparency and oversight provide opportunities for organized crime to gain influence over elected officials by financing their campaigns."[46]

Haiti's legislation regarding political financing is forward-looking as it stipulates that 50 percent of the public funds that parties receive must be used for the political education of party members and to support women's electoral contests. However, the enforcement of this law and its impact on the political culture has left much to be desired. The efforts to strengthen the political parties are yet to produce the expected results, as fragmentation and poor party self-regulation remain predominant.

In a document published in 2005, "From Grassroots to the Airwaves: Paying for Political Parties and Campaigns in the Caribbean," the OAS Inter-American Forum on Political Parties addressed the situation of political finance in Haiti.

This document states, "Political debate in Haiti does not focus on political party financing, but instead revolves around security and the continuing national political crisis. While the Constitution mandates the creation of a Permanent Electoral Council that ostensibly would monitor the financing of political parties, circumstances have not permitted its establishment. Since 1990, three provisional electoral councils have been constituted to organize and supervise elections that were often called on an ad hoc basis outside of the timeline mandated by the Constitution. Likewise, there is no tradition of transparency regarding the

[46] "Funding of Political Parties and Election Campaigns: A Handbook on Political Finance | International IDEA."

utilization of public funds. According to noted historian Leslie J. R. Péan, "the State is perceived as the private property of those in power, and public funds are administered accordingly.[47]"

Public funding of political parties and elections could be an important link in the chain of a stable and well-run political system. However, it takes the stakeholders' commitment, competence, and integrity to produce the expected results. Again, an educated population and well-trained civil servants and political leaders are imperative for democracy to flourish and contribute to equitable prosperity.

Therefore, a massive effort to develop the minds and raise the literacy and social level of the Haitian people is a must. As syndicated columnist Jonah Goldberg pointed out, focusing on and developing Haiti's "intangible assets" such as skills, rule of law, knowledge, favorable customs, high expectations, integrity, and trust is imperative. These drivers generate and sustain a prosperous society. The real wealth of nations is found not in factories, oil deposits, and gold mines but in the citizens' minds, hearts, dispositions, and habits. Timeless principles and values ingrained in intangible assets are wealth per se and transmute into more and more wealth over time. Overlooking them carries tragic consequences.[48]

In its study, "Where is the Wealth of the Nations, Measuring Capital in the 21st Century," the World Bank states, "Worldwide, natural capital (cropland, pastureland, and protected areas) accounts for 5 percent of total wealth, produced capital (buildings, machinery, equipment, and infrastructure) for 18 percent, and intangible capital for 77 percent.[49]"

In light of the importance of intangible assets, any nation-building program must seek to build the capacity and enrich the minds of a critical mass in the population. Without this

[47] "Grassroots.Pdf."
[48] "Tough Love Needed for Haiti | National Review."
[49] "Where Is the Wealth of Nations?: Measuring Capital for the 21st Century."

foundational step, no structure or system will stand and thrive in the long run, as they will be corrupted, neglected, or vandalized.

Nation-building in Haiti, as everywhere else, is a complex venture and may look like a catch-22. However, the emergence of visionary and servant leaders may be the starting point of it all. Such leaders understand that nation-building is first and foremost about building trust, inspiring people to improve themselves daily, promoting and teaching core principles and values that sustain any human enterprise, and showing the mountaintop people can reach. Success in leadership will start a virtuous cycle that takes society to leaps and bounds for the greater good. Therefore, pursuing trust in the governance system, studying, promoting, and practicing effective leadership must permeate every state institution, initiative, and policy. Gaps in leadership will jeopardize the best plans, turn governing into navigation by sight, and make social harmony an elusive target.

For too long, leaders in Haiti have fallen prey to what Plato described as the Ring of Gyges. Gyges, one of the shepherds of the king of Lydia, realized that he could become invisible by turning inward the collet of a ring he ran into by chance during a violent storm that had opened the ground before him. With the awareness of his new power, he arranged to be part of the messengers sent to the royal palace. There, thanks to his capacity for invisibility, he seduced the queen, conspired with her, killed the king, and took over the kingdom.

This story points out that an impunity-conscious man will do anything to satisfy his interests if there are no immediate and major negative consequences. *"Gyges did not use his new skills to serve the community, protect the weak and orphans, and promote justice. He only dreamed of satisfying his personal ambitions, even if he had to overthrow the established order.*[50]*"*

Engulfed in the Gyges syndrome culture, Haitian elites have lost sight of the "Ford factor" or long-term benefit of lifting the

[50] "Gyges-a.Pdf."

downtrodden, so they have a vested interest and the wherewithal to support the established order. In fact, history has reported plethoric cases of pilfering the state coffers through corruption, bogus contracts, or dubious methods to protect monopolies or business advantages, thus depriving the state of the means to improve the condition of the population.

The task of changing the attitude of an elite is, at best, complex. International sanctions can help as deterrents and call attention to possible consequences. However, if within the country, despite the sanctions, the embezzlers keep enjoying their loot with impunity and continue to exercise their corrupting influence, the result of any foreign effort will be very limited. Further unintended consequences deriving from foreign sanctions may stifle business and the country's development process. If a critical mass of businesspeople is involved in wrongdoing, restrictions on their capacity to make international transactions will affect the flow of basic goods to the masses. This issue is a conundrum, as doing nothing will do more harm in the long run.

Motivational speaker Jim Rohn said, "Not long ago, I did a seminar for a group of oil company executives during their convention in Honolulu. While we were sitting around the conference table, one of them asked, 'Mr. Rohn, you know some important people around the world. What do you think the next ten years will be like?' I said, 'Gentlemen, I do know the right people. I can tell you.' So, they all listened very carefully. I said, 'Gentlemen, based on the people I know and from the best of my own experience, I've concluded that in the coming ten years, things are going to be about like they've always been.'" Then Rohn added, "Someone says, 'Well, then, how will my life change?' And the answer is when you change."

Knowing that the elites in Haiti will do what they have always done, the question is: How can Haiti develop itself without supportive elites? This question takes us back to the vital importance and transformative impact of servant leadership. It takes an accountable and visionary leader with a mission and a keen sense of justice to steer their people through the process of nation-building or recovery from survival-threatening crises.

Many leaders in Haiti seem to nurture the naïve philosophy that their bad actions would have no negative consequences. For them the law of sowing and reaping is an ethereal concept with no grounding in life reality. They seek to bear fruit without caring for the roots. Thus, they defy the universe's natural laws and bring disaster upon themselves and the country.

Philip Freeman, in the book "How to Run a Country: An Ancient Guide for Modern Leaders," presented Marcus Tullius Cicero's ideas about country governance. One of Cicero's cardinal thoughts was, "There are universal laws that govern the conduct of human affairs." Studying and leading by these laws offer a dependable track for success and great achievements in the process of nation-building.

Among the natural laws governing nation-building, Freeman highlighted the following:

The best form of government embraces a balance of powers. Even the most noble kings will become tyrants if their reign is unchecked, just as democracy will degrade into mob rule without constraints on popular power. A just government must be founded on a system of checks and balances. Beware the leader who sets aside constitutional rules claiming the need for expediency or security.

Corruption destroys a nation. Greed, bribery, and fraud devour a country from the inside, leaving it weak and vulnerable. Corruption is not merely a moral evil, but a practical menace that leaves citizens at best disheartened, at worst seething with anger and ripe for revolution.

The laws of a state rule over a leader just as he rules over the people. Indeed, we could say that a leader is the voice of the law, and the law is a silent leader. The rule of government should be in harmony with justice and the fundamental principles of nature, by which I mean it is in agreement with law.

Also, Cicero pointed out the overarching goal country leaders must pursue, saying, *"What destination should those steering the Republic keep their eyes fixed upon and by what course should they guide us there? The answer is what the most reasonable, decent, and blessed people always desire: peace with honor."*

In politics, it is irresponsible to take an unwavering stand when circumstances are always evolving, and good men change their minds. Clinging to the same opinion no matter the cost has never been considered a virtue among statesmen.[51]

How can a nation develop and renew a cadre of political servant leaders to steer the ship of state? As mentioned, a political system may be sturdy and have proved effective in many countries, but in other political ecosystems, the men at its helm can easily plot to corrupt it for personal gains or to perpetuate themselves in power, as has been observed repeatedly in Haiti. Laws, principles, and values do not and cannot stand by themselves. The best policies that have worked miracles in developed countries will be unfruitful in other countries without men and women who have prepared themselves for high responsibilities and have a sense of mission.

Leadership building remains at the heart of the nation-building process. Preparing effective leaders must be a deliberate and constant pursuit. Developed countries take seriously the responsibility of shaping future leaders and set up academic institutions to nurture the leadership training process from generation to generation.

In the United States, Ivy League universities are breeding grounds for political leaders, top businessmen, and social transformers. Jacob Morgan, author of The Future Leader, pointed out that many US billionaires and successful politicians "went to Ivy League schools, such as Elon Musk at UPenn and Jeff Bezos at Harvard. Nearly half of all U.S. presidents went to Ivy

[51] Cicero, How to Run a Country.

League schools, and 8 out of 9 members of the U.S. Supreme Court went to Yale or Harvard.[52]"

In France, General Charles de Gaulle established the École Nationale d'Administration (ENA) in 1945 to attract the best possible talents into the public administration, pull the public service from corruption and inefficiency, and change a system of patronage and spoils. This school has trained many presidents, prime ministers, business executives, and social leaders. Recently, President Emmanuel Macron has undertaken restructuring and renaming the school to inject more equity and inclusiveness in the admission process and address the nagging perception of elitism that has stuck so long to public opinion.

In Singapore, the LKY School seeks to develop thought leadership, improve standards of governance, and transform lives for a greater projection of the country's influence in the world.

Visionary and servant leadership is not a spontaneous generation. It must be envisioned, planned, promoted, and nurtured. Without this kind of leadership, the best political systems flounder, good constitutions remain empty rhetoric, and the best minds find their way toward better horizons, thus fueling the brain drain phenomenon. Therefore, a deliberate framework and assiduous efforts must be invested into the process of producing transformational leadership.

It is true that a critical mass of well-trained civil servants can optimize the delivery of services to the population and steer economic and social policies. However, it takes competent and committed heads of state and government, ministers, permanent secretaries, and other high-level officers to enforce the rules, sustain equity, and boost morale.

Wise King Solomon said, "Woe to you, O land, when your king is childish, and your princes feast in the morning. Blessed are you, O land, when your king is the son of nobility, and your princes feast at the proper time, with self-control and not in

[52] Morgan, The Future Leader.

drunkenness." (Eccl 10: 16-17 NET). This passage is a testament to the vital role of proper leadership. Misfortune overtakes the land where leaders don't assume their responsibility, don't take their role seriously, and engage in an epicurean lifestyle of pride, corruption, and a rigid and uncompromising attitude.

King Solomon provided a vivid description of the root cause of Haiti's downward spiral. History confirms his sage observation. When Toussaint Louverture provided quality leadership, he placed the land on the right track and fostered a cadre of generals who worked out a unique feat in universal history. Henri Christophe provided quality leadership to Haiti's northern kingdom, and his jurisdiction prospered. La Citadelle Laferrière attests to Christophe's visionary and shrewd governance. When power became an end in itself, and leaders relied on force, exclusive governance, and resource grabbing, the country found itself on an unending slippery slope.

Leaders set the tone and exert a huge impact on the administrative culture. If a head of state engages in a luxurious lifestyle, laid-back attitude, goalless missions abroad for the sake of traveling, and epicurean habits, his ministers will take a page from his book and emulate him; other high-level officers will take a cue from their example and take their work lightly. In no time, ethics will be sent to the back seat, visions of a prosperous and equitable future will be clouded, and opportunism will reign supreme. In such a rotten moral and political environment, the down and out in society are left to fend for themselves, the government loses legitimacy, the population loses confidence in its leaders, and unprincipled and reckless men rise without resistance from law-abiding citizens and shake the foundations of the social edifice.

Weak leadership makes weak economies and weak nations. Robust leadership makes robust economies and robust nations. Even in the best cases, steering the ship of state is a tall order, let alone in man-made, inconducive circumstances. To top it all, no other country can override the influence of leaders to induce necessary changes. Therefore, the proper and continuous training of leaders and a political system that facilitates their emergence is key to sustaining the process of nation-building and socio-economic development.

CHAPTER 8
REFORMING STATE INSTITUTIONS

Nothing is possible without men, but nothing lasts without institutions.
Jean Monnet, diplomat and statesman

The foundation of any thriving nation lies in its governance system and the efficiency of its institutions, particularly its public administration. The journey toward stable governance and a robust public administration in Haiti will nurture the dream of a transformed country. One that stands as a beacon of hope and progress is not beyond reach.

In the words of the Economist Douglas North, "Institutions are the rules of the game in a society, . . . the humanly devised constraints that shape human interaction. . . . They structure incentives in human exchange, whether political, social or economic.[53]" Institutions include contracts and contract enforcement, protection of property rights, the rule of law, government bureaucracies, and financial markets. They also include habits, beliefs, norms, social cleavages, and traditions. Formal institutions typically tend to crystallize informal institutions.

Institution building in Haiti is akin to orchestrating a symphony. Each branch of government, be it judicial, legislative, or executive, is an instrument, contributing its unique sound to the nation's harmony. The challenge and opportunity lie in tuning

[53] North, Institutions, Institutional Change and Economic Performance.

these instruments to play in concert so that they resonate with the aspirations of the Haitian people. The transformational power of institution building is not a mere theoretical proposition; it is a reality witnessed across the globe. From the rebuilding of post-war societies to the economic miracles in Asia, history is replete with tales of nations that have risen from the ashes through the strength of their institutions.

The renaissance of Haiti begins with the critical task of rebuilding the governance system and establishing robust institutions. With sustainable reforms, the vision is clear: a Haiti where transparent, accountable, and efficient governance paves the way for national prosperity and international confidence.

Overcoming stumbling blocks to institutional viability requires desiring and envisioning a reformed governance system that embodies the principles of good governance: transparency, accountability, participation, and efficiency. These principles are not merely aspirational but the bedrock upon which a resilient and responsive government is built. The attendant trust between the government and the population will create an environment where people feel empowered to participate in the governance process and hold their leaders accountable.

Transforming this vision into reality requires a holistic approach that will chart the course to modernizing public administration through digital transformation, capacity building, and efficient resource management.

Under the amended 1987 Constitution, Haiti's governance system operates as a semi-presidential republic featuring an executive branch led by the president and the prime minister, a bicameral legislature, and an independent judiciary. However, this formal structure faces significant practical challenges. Many government institutions are chronically underfunded and lack capacity, leading to inefficient public services. Despite its theoretical independence, the judiciary often lacks resources and autonomy, resulting in low public confidence.

Envisioning a reformed governance system for Haiti begins with tapping the transformative power of good governance principles. These principles sustain a governance system that can earn the trust and support of the population while fostering national development.

Transparency is the bedrock of a trustworthy governance system. It entails open decision-making processes, accessible information, and clear communication channels between the government and the population. Adopting transparency means implementing policies that mandate the disclosure of government activities, budgets, and contracts. This openness curbs corruption and empowers citizens to hold their leaders accountable. In transparency, decisions are made in the public eye, reducing the space for corrupt practices and fostering a culture of integrity.

Accountability is closely linked to transparency and is essential for a functioning democracy. It requires mechanisms that ensure government officials are answerable for their actions and decisions. This can be achieved through independent oversight bodies and the enforcement of stringent anti-corruption laws without political interference. Public institutions' regular audits and performance reviews can also help identify inefficiencies and promote accountability. These mechanisms can ensure that the governance system operates with a high level of integrity and responsibility.

Participation is the cornerstone of inclusive governance. It involves actively engaging citizens in decision-making and ensuring their voices are heard and considered. Enhancing public participation in Haiti means creating platforms for dialogue between the government and its citizens. This engagement can be achieved through town hall meetings, public consultations, and digital platforms facilitating direct communication with policymakers. Encouraging the participation of marginalized groups, including women, youth, and rural communities, is crucial for achieving equitable governance. A participatory culture leads to a more inclusive and representative governance system that reflects its population's diverse needs and aspirations.

Efficiency in governance ensures that public resources are used optimally to deliver quality services to citizens. This means modernizing public administration through the adoption of e-governance and digital transformation. Implementing digital tools can streamline administrative processes, reduce bureaucratic red tape, and improve service delivery for the benefit of all Haitians.

A robust public administration in Haiti provides a foundation for effectively implementing governance reforms and delivering essential services to the population. A modernized and efficient public administration system can significantly enhance the government's capacity to respond to citizens' needs, promote economic development, and strengthen the overall governance framework.

Public administration is the conveyor belt for implementing vision, policies, and decisions. No matter how well-intentioned a government, success will remain elusive without the continuing development of civil servants, improved work conditions, adequate structures, standard procedures, a culture of accountability, and adapted tools and technology. No farmer can expect to reap abundant crops without a knowledgeable and motivated team, good seeds, fertilizers, pesticides, effective equipment, and hope for cashing in on the harvest. No head of state or government can expect to transform Haiti without a functional and effective administration.

In 2022, Haiti had 107,155 civil servants for a population of almost twelve million. According to the 2021 Report on the Workforce of the Public Function in Haiti published by the Office of Management and Human Resources (OMRH):

> *The number of civil servants per capita in Haiti is low. It amounts to 8 civil servants per 1,000 inhabitants. This indicator shows that Haiti is an under-administered country. The low number of civil servants per inhabitant causes inadequate service provision for the*

population. Compared to other countries in Latin America and the Caribbean, taken as a sample, Haiti is ranked last considering the number of civil servants per capita. Next come Chile (19/1000), the Dominican Republic (34/1000), Mexico (40/1000), Paraguay (43/1000), Costa Rica (53/1000), and Argentina, with the highest number of civil servants per inhabitant at 76 per 1000 inhabitants.

Comparing these data with some OECD countries, the trend remains the same, with the gap widening. Spain, the United States, Great Britain, and France have 61, 69, 78, and 90 civil servants per 1,000 inhabitants respectively. These comparative data show how much Haiti is under-administered, with only 8 civil servants per 1000 inhabitants. This weakness constitutes a major obstacle preventing Haiti from meeting the needs of her population.[54]

How can Haiti expect to pull it off with most of her development indicators in the red and trailing most countries worldwide? Two considerations place Haiti in the right position to bounce back from the abyss. As author Napoleon Hill said, "*Every adversity, every failure, every heartache carries the seed of an equal or greater benefit.*[55]" The country fell from the enviable position of an economic powerhouse and freedom flag bearer. Therefore, the unspeakable adversity afflicting society can be a springboard for reaching new heights with visionary and servant leadership, effective justice systems, and universal education.

One of the practical steps in modernizing public administration is the adoption of e-governance and digital transformation. Many Haitian government offices operate with outdated technology and inefficient paper-based systems. Digital platforms streamline administrative processes. For example, an integrated digital system for managing public records, issuing permits, and processing applications can drastically reduce processing times and increase transparency.

In addition to digital transformation, streamlined

---

[54] "Rfph_201802.Pdf."
[55] Hill and Pell, Think and Grow Rich.

administrative processes involve conducting comprehensive reviews of existing procedures to identify and eliminate redundancies and inefficiencies. Simplified workflows, standardized procedures, and clear guidelines can help make public services more accessible and user-friendly. For instance, one-stop service centers where citizens can access multiple government services in a single location can significantly enhance convenience and efficiency.

Further, effective resource allocation and management will ensure that public administration can function optimally and respond to the population's needs. First, improving budget management practices should be prioritized. Haiti needs modern budgeting techniques, such as program-based budgeting, which links funding allocations to specific outcomes and performance indicators. Such an approach will help use resources efficiently to achieve desired results. Additionally, robust financial oversight mechanisms, including regular audits and transparent reporting, will enhance accountability and prevent the misuse of public funds.

Second, securing adequate funding for critical public services and infrastructure is vital. This may involve exploring innovative financing mechanisms, such as public-private partnerships, to supplement government resources. For example, partnering with private sector companies to develop and maintain infrastructure projects like roads and telecommunications networks can help bridge the funding gap and improve service delivery.

Learning from the experiences of other countries provides invaluable insights and practical strategies for reforming governance and public administration in Haiti. Successful reforms occurred in various nations, with practices that can be adapted to Haiti's context to achieve tangible improvements in governance and public service delivery.

Estonia, a small Baltic nation, has become a global leader in e-governance through its ambitious digital transformation initiatives. Faced with the need to rebuild its public administration after gaining independence in the early 1990s, Estonia embraced technology to create a more efficient and transparent government. The country introduced a comprehensive e-governance system that allows citizens to access a wide range of public services online, from registering businesses to voting in elections.

One key component of Estonia's success is X-Road, a secure data exchange platform that connects various government databases and enables seamless information sharing between public institutions. This system has significantly reduced bureaucratic red tape and improved service delivery. Haiti can learn from Estonia's experience by investing in digital infrastructure and developing integrated platforms for public service delivery. Such systems can streamline administrative processes, enhance transparency, and make government services more accessible to citizens.

Rwanda is another encouraging example; this country has achieved incredible progress in development and governance and can teach us a lot about fighting corruption. Rwanda put strong anti-corruption measures in place to restore public institutions' credibility following the terrible genocide in 1994. Significantly lower levels of corruption resulted from the government's introduction and strict enforcement of anti-corruption laws. Public officials must disclose their assets, and those found guilty of corrupt activities face severe punishments from the government. Additionally, Rwanda has fostered a culture of openness by giving the public easy access to government data.

Haiti can take comparable steps by bolstering its anti-corruption organizations, like the Unit for the Fight Against Corruption (ULCC), and ensuring they have the autonomy and funding necessary to function efficiently. Strict sanctions for corruption and enforcing asset declaration laws can discourage corrupt behavior and increase public confidence in governmental institutions.

In keeping with the principle of transparency, the city of Porto Alegre in Brazil used participatory budgeting. This system has demonstrated its ability to allocate resources and successfully engage citizens in transparent decision-making processes. Residents can vote on community budget priorities and take part in discussions. The approach results in equal resource distribution and increased public satisfaction with government services.

Participatory budgeting can help Haiti at the municipal and national levels. By incorporating individuals in budgetary choices, the government can guarantee that resources are distributed according to the population's needs and priorities. This participatory approach enhances transparency and accountability, as citizens can directly observe and influence how public funds are spent.

Singapore's situation is remarkable. This nation's success in creating an efficient public administration may be mainly ascribed to its focus on professional growth for public servants. The Civil Service College offers continuous training and development programs for government workers. The courses focus on acquiring knowledge in digital literacy, policy analysis, and leadership.

Haiti can apply this concept by grouping sectoral or specialized training programs for public personnel and offering continuous opportunities for professional growth. By ensuring that government staff members receive ongoing education and training, which raises their competency and promotes service delivery, the public administration can meet the requirements of modern governance and the expectations of its constituency.

Implementing governance and public administration reforms calls for a clear, staged approach that meets urgent needs while laying the foundation for sustainable, long-term developments. A well-crafted road map should show the actions and policies required to redesign Haiti's government systems, ensuring that every stage advances the one before it.

Establishing the fundamental elements of a successful reform should take center stage in the first phase. Digital infrastructure and an efficient public service delivery system should be on the front burner. Financial agencies need significant resources, training, legal power, and pilot projects for participatory budgeting in certain towns to produce better outcomes. This will help increase public involvement.

The second phase can concentrate on short-term reforms to produce low-hanging fruit. At this stage, the government will roll out integrated digital systems across all main services. Public servants will need clear guidelines and standard procedures to use these new systems, and service users must be aware of online access. Ensuring the system's success through constant monitoring and evaluation with necessary corrections guarantees its efficiency.

Legal reforms during this period are quite important. They include strengthening independent monitoring agencies and using judicial review systems. Constant professional growth for judges and court employees guarantees judicial independence and the rule of law. Moreover, improved civic education initiatives for growing inclusivity will enlighten people about their rights, the need to vote, and how to participate in governance.

The medium-term phase strives to consolidate past accomplishments and extend the reforms. Building capacity in major government institutions involves providing resources and expertise to ensure their effectiveness. Good performance management calls for periodic evaluation and unambiguous indicators to encourage accountability. Recruitment and promotion of public officials under a transparent, merit-based system will likely produce a qualified and driven workforce.

Feedback channels will allow the public service operators to assess the effectiveness of policies and procedures, identifying and addressing deficiencies. Partnership with international organizations, donor agencies, and other countries can help with continuous adaptation by providing technical assistance, financing, and best practices.

These changes require collaboration for a transparent, responsible, and efficient governing system, paving the way for a prosperous and inclusive future. The suggested institutional reforms will help improve public involvement, fight corruption, and strengthen the judicial branch. They are likely to solve the long-standing national systemic deficiencies.

Although international support and collaboration can offer standards and best practices, Haiti's success depends on its will to reform and change. Effective nation-building and growth require transparent and predictable legal and administrative frameworks.

Regarding the enforcement of quality rules, American political scientist Francis Fukuyama wrote in "State-Building: Governance and World Order in the 21st Century," "Strong states did not merely protect the rule of law, but they enforced laws that laid the groundwork for economic growth, provided goods and services that private actors could not, and knitted citizens into a single nation.[56]"

Luca Ferrini wrote an important thesis on "The Importance of Institutions to Economic Development." In it he argued that cross-country empirical analyses, in combination with micro-level studies, provide strong support for the overwhelming importance of institutions in predicting the level of development in countries around the world. Protection of property rights, effective law enforcement, and efficient bureaucracies, together with a broad range of norms and civic mores, are found to be strongly correlated to better economic performance over time[57]. As Haiti engages on its path of institution building, it will stand as a lighthouse of hope, not just for its people but for the world.

[56] Fukuyama, State Building.
[57] Ferrini, "The Importance of Institutions to Economic Development."

CHAPTER 9
JUSTICE WILL TRANSFORM HAITI

Doing what is right makes a nation great, but sin will bring disgrace to any people. Prov 14:34

Justice is an essential component of a prosperous society. It protects rights, dignity, and respect for all individuals and upholds the rule of law over the rule of might. To achieve transformation in Haiti, citizens must embrace these ideas and work towards a fair society where everyone has a voice and a stake in the country's future.

Fairness, equality, natural law, ethics, and reason are foundations for justice. They imply that rights are protected and wrongs are addressed through proper legal channels. A fair society guarantees every citizen the same legal opportunities and protections regardless of socioeconomic status, skin color, or background.

The advent of an effective justice system in Haiti will promote social development by protecting individuals' rights and freedoms, ensuring equal treatment under the law, and addressing grievances fairly. Those who feel their legal rights are safeguarded are more likely to engage in civic activities, grow their neighborhood, and advance social peace. People feel safe and valuable in a society that supports mutual respect and a sense of belonging.

Haiti's political and economic success rests on a strong legal system. Such a system guarantees agreements, safeguards property rights, offers the framework required for corporate operations, and fairly handles conflicts. Legal consistency promotes economic progress, attracts domestic and international capital, and spurs entrepreneurship. When companies and entrepreneurs feel the law will protect their investments and inventions, they are more willing to fund long-term projects and support sustainable economic development.

Justice guarantees public officials' accountability and protects the democratic process, leading to political stability. A fair legal system checks the government, prevents corruption and abuse of power, and increases public confidence in political institutions. People who believe the judicial system is fair and objective are more likely to get involved in politics.

Justice will help lower crime and violence because people will rely on legal procedures rather than extrajudicial means to address their issues. An open judicial process will demystify the legal system's complexity and enable the general public to access and understand it, reducing dependence on superstition. Transparent and widely accessible court procedures and rulings strengthen public confidence and social harmony. People are less inclined to perpetrate crimes when they know they will be held accountable and face consequences.

An effective governance system applies social and economic fairness to solve the underlying causes of violence and crime—poverty, social marginalization, and illiteracy. Social justice guarantees that every person has equal access and opportunities, thereby reducing the contributing factors to illicit behaviors and enabling peaceful resolution of interpersonal conflicts.

Using restorative justice and giving rehabilitation and peace top priority instead of retributive legal action pays dividends. Restorative justice can greatly lower recidivism and advance long-term social stability. It prioritizes the community, perpetrators, and victims' participation, improving harmony and is likely to lower crime rates.

Effective law enforcement and policing are prerequisites for a just society since they show that illegal acts carry harsh consequences and help build public confidence by enhancing public safety. Studies of community policing initiatives that connect with local citizens to help solve their security issues have demonstrated that they lower crime rates and improve social cohesion.

The five justice pillars—fairness, equality, responsibility, transparency, and accessibility—together create a thorough framework that protects the rights of every person and preserves the rule of law in a transformed Haiti. These pillars are interlocking and mutually reinforcing.

While fairness and equality assure equal treatment of all people, responsibility and openness help to build confidence in the system. Accessibility guarantees that justice is a right rather than a privilege, a common good at the disposal of everyone. These pillars create a strong structure supporting the rule of law and a justice culture.

Justice, in all its expressions—distributive, retributive, procedural, restorative—will flourish in a society where everyone has opportunities. Haiti's transformation depends on a clear roadmap to implementing these facets.

Haiti's judicial system is structured into court levels. The Courts of First Instance (lower courts) handle most civil and criminal matters and are the system's backbone. For most people looking for justice, these courts represent their first point of contact.

The Courts of Appeal review lower courts' rulings to guarantee legal accuracy and equity.

The Cour de Cassation (Supreme Court) is at the pinnacle of the judicial hierarchy. It serves as the final arbiter of legal disputes and has the authority to interpret the Constitution.

Haiti also has specialized courts, such as labor and land courts, that address specific legal issues. The system includes "peace tribunals" for minor infractions. The Ministry of Justice and Public Security oversees the legal system, working with the Haitian National Police to guarantee public order and execute court rulings.

Article 184.2 of the Amended 1987 Constitution stipulates, "The Administration and the control of the Judicial Branch is entrusted to a High Council of the Judicial Branch (Conseil Supérieur du Pouvoir Judiciaire) who exercises over judges a right of supervision and discipline, and who has a general power of information and recommendation on the state of the Judiciary."

Notwithstanding this organized framework, the Haitian court system struggles for credibility and efficiency. Corruption has undermined public confidence and eroded the impartial administration of justice. Case rulings often are based on bribery, nepotism, and interference from powerful people rather than on legal grounds. Systemic corruption causes unequal treatment of people since those with financial means or connections can take advantage of the system, therefore depriving the most vulnerable without access.

The court's credibility has to be rebuilt, and its efficacy improved. The legal procedure around the murder of President Jovenel Moïse serves as an example of the obstacles compromising the foundations of justice in Haiti. More than three years after the magnicide, none of the suspects have been judged. Yet on the first anniversary of the assassination, four judges had recused themselves shortly after being assigned the case. What may ordinary citizens expect from the judiciary?

Corruption claims, political intervention, and inefficiency have all slowed the probe. Despite the case's high profile, progress has been slow, with major suspects still at large and evidence allegedly mishandled or ignored. Inefficiency has undermined public confidence in the legal system, leading many Haitians to believe that justice is unduly delayed or denied. The legal procedure's lack of openness and accountability begs questions regarding the justice system's capacity to uphold the rule of law.

The initial arrests and ensuing treatment of suspects have prompted questions regarding the fairness of the legal treatment of all parties involved. There have been allegations that individuals with political connections or financial resources have been able to elude justice, while those without such influence receive more severe scrutiny and treatment. This perceived disparity undermines the principle of equality and underscores the systemic issues of corruption and bias that afflict Haiti's judicial system.

The ongoing investigation of President Moïse's murder serves as a stark reminder of the imperative necessity for comprehensive judicial reforms to reestablish trust in Haiti's legal institutions and guarantee that justice is truly accessible to all.

The United States judiciary has made significant progress in investigating the assassination of President Jovenel Moïse. The US has successfully prosecuted and convicted several conspirators.

Rodolphe Jaar, a dual citizen of Haiti and Chile, received a federal prison sentence after pleading guilty to providing material assistance for the killing. Mario Antonio Palacios, a former Colombian soldier, was also sentenced to life. Furthermore, On December 19, 2023, former senator John Joel Joseph, extradited from Jamaica in May 2022, was sentenced to life in federal prison after entering a plea of guilty to three charges, including conspiring to murder and kidnap an individual outside the United States and providing material support and resources to execute the conspiracy to kill President Moise.

The US judiciary's rapid and decisive actions, including successful prosecution and transparent legal proceedings, starkly contrast Haiti's sluggish and complex judicial process. The US legal system's efforts highlight the necessity of an independent court in providing justice and defending the rule of law, even in complex and politically sensitive matters.

The 2007 International Crisis Group (ICG) briefing, titled "Haiti: Justice Reform and the Security Crisis," is scathing. The group states:

The judiciary is encumbered by incompetence and corruption, partly due to inadequate pay, infrastructure, and logistical support. The legal code is antiquated, barely modified since Napoleon bequeathed it to the one-time French colony; judges are not independent; case management is poor; and indigent defendants rarely have counsel. The state can guarantee neither the security of its citizens nor the rights of defendants. When arrests are made, the system is virtually incapable of conducting trials. Prisons become more crowded, and street crime escalates daily while court procedures move at a snail's pace. The results are prolonged pre-trial detention, lack of due process, and near-total absence of public confidence in the criminal justice system.[58]

Political interference and impunity reign supreme. Many politicians recklessly pilfered the PetroCaribe money accumulated from a scheme in which the late Venezuelan president, Hugo Chávez, allowed the proceeds of oil product sales to be used for development purposes and be paid in the future at a low interest rate. The justice system has been weaponized to the point that law-abiding citizens have been kidnapped, murdered, robbed, or raped under the indifferent watch of established authorities. Persistent public outcry suggests that many of these authorities are in cahoots with gangs that terrorize the population.

The only way to address this grave situation is through collective reeducation in democracy and civics. Justice is more than just enforcing laws; it is the foundation for a society's growth and prosperity. It ensures that all citizens, regardless of background, skin color, or status, have an equal chance to live with dignity, fairness, and security.

The Holy Scriptures say, "Doing what is right makes a nation great" (Prov 14: 34). These words chart a course for Haiti in its quest to attain unity, social harmony, and an economic breakthrough. Justice holds a transformative power and will catalyze a brighter future for Haiti.

---

[58] "Haiti: Justice Reform and the Security Crisis | Crisis Group."

In Petite Rivière de l'Artibonite, my father cultivated a thriving farm that was a testament to his hard work and dedication. His fields flourished, feeding not only our family but the local community as well. Nevertheless, the resentment of others increased in tandem with his success. The whispers of resentment soon transformed into threats and conspiracy, compelling him to temporarily depart the land where he had invested his life and passion. As the threats emanated from individuals he had previously regarded as his neighbors, the betrayal caused him immense pain.

Determined to resist intimidation, my father returned to his farm. Then, he faced more difficulties as troublemakers and crooks tried to invade his land. Still yearning for justice, he battled in the courtroom. Corruption and delays compromised what should have been a straightforward process. He had to incur excessive expenses for bailiffs, attorneys, court clerks, and extensive documentation. He also had to navigate a maze of complex and ineffectual procedures. Despite emotional and financial challenges, my father persevered and presented his case in multiple courts until the Court of Cassation, which remained mute, leaving it limbo.

My father persevered through the stumbling blocks. He refused to let the avarice of others define him and lessen his rights. Like my father, I dream of a Haiti where just laws enable communities to flourish, law-abiding people are treated properly, and injustice is no longer a hindrance to development.

We must streamline the legal system, engage with the communities, and strategically use technology to achieve justice. These changes will result in an egalitarian, effective, and transparent legal system that serves all citizens. Modernizing and streamlining the judiciary is vital for Haiti's development. Justice corrects wrongdoings, advances political and economic stability, and strengthens social cohesion.

The legal system must effectively deter offenders and corrupt officials. Independent bodies such as the High Council of Magistracy (CSM) and the High Council of the Judicial Branch (CSPJ) should be reinforced to investigate corruption, properly monitor judicial operations, and apply severe penalties for transgression.

Clear, merit-based recruiting and career management policies for judges can greatly help counter political intervention and nepotism. Furthermore, mandating regular disclosure of assets and financial interests among all court officials will help increase openness and uncover any inexplicable wealth suggesting corruption.

Judges, prosecutors, and court officials require ongoing professional development programs to enhance their legal knowledge, ethical standards, and procedural skills. This training should adopt international standards to ensure the court is up-to-date on global best practices.

Specialized training emphasizing the significance of impartiality, ethics, and integrity in the judicial process will contribute to establishing a culture of accountability and honesty within the judiciary. Capacity-building initiatives, including workshops, seminars, and exchange programs with other countries, can further strengthen the skills and perspectives of judicial staff.

Improving Haiti's court system infrastructure is also critical. Modernizing and renovating courthouse buildings will help establish an appropriate court process setting. Every courthouse must have the required tools and apply modern technologies like computerized case management systems and digital documents. An online database helps to reduce the likelihood of missing or altered documents and increases efficiency.

Moreover, increasing the number of legal aid centers — especially in rural and underdeveloped areas—will ensure that everyone can access legal advice and assistance. Community participation will help reform the justice system. Public awareness campaigns enable individuals to understand and exercise their legal rights. These efforts could use TV and radio shows, and social media to appeal to more beneficiaries. Civil society groups (CSOs) will provide legal aid to vulnerable people, monitor the legal system, and advocate improvements.

Local mediation centers and other community-based justice initiatives can also resolve small disputes, thereby relieving official court burden. These services can promote social cohesion through conflict resolution based on dialogue and compromise. Training courses on legal literacy and fundamental legal procedures will help local volunteers and community leaders by equipping them with the knowledge they need to advocate for justice and help others navigate the legal system.

Technology will improve openness, efficiency, and accessibility in Haiti's court system. An online case management system will allow the public and legal professionals to monitor case status in real time. Legal documents, court decisions, and procedural guidelines will be widely available, demystifying the legal system's complexity.

Another innovative approach is to make justice available through mobile legal services. Advanced mobile legal service units can provide legal assistance in remote areas. These departments can aid with documentation, legal advice, and communication with the formal legal system. Creating user-friendly e-government platforms with integrated public services, including legal services, can provide residents with a one-stop shop for assistance and information.

International cooperation can help Haiti strengthen its justice system by sharing resources, knowledge, and best practices. Forming international alliances and learning from effective legal reform initiatives in other nations would help Haiti establish an efficient judiciary. Haitian officials will benefit from working with specialists from other countries to develop and implement reforms. Small actions can make a potent impact in creating a more egalitarian Haiti. Prompt and well-thought-out measures promote a culture that values dignity and respect for all citizens, upholds the rule of law, and prioritizes justice for national development and peace.

Nelson Mandela's encouraging remarks show that legal reform can happen: "*Until it is done, it always seems impossible.*" Haitians can make justice a reality and change their nation by acting tenaciously, deliberately, and collectively.

CHAPTER 10

UPLIFTING THE SANCTITY OF LIFE, HUMAN DIGNITY, AND HUMAN RIGHTS

The rights of every man are diminished when the rights of one man are threatened. John F. Kennedy, former US president

The sanctity of life, human dignity, and human rights are essential for establishing peace and prosperity. Human rights are the foundation of a fair society. They ensure everyone will be treated with respect, equity, and compassion. Protecting and promoting human rights is pragmatic and ethical in order to achieve long-term peace and progress.

Haiti struggles greatly to uphold human rights despite its vibrant culture and indomitable will. Chronic political unrest, economic challenges, and social inequity have plagued the country and made it a place where human rights violations happen too often. A quick and thorough response is imperative for many people to get basic education and medical care, live free from violence and exploitation.

Haiti can improve respect for human rights. International mechanisms and instruments provide standard frameworks in this regard. The Universal Declaration of Human Rights (UDHR) and the Inter-American Commission on Human Rights (IACHR) offer guidance and support for people to exercise their rights. Thus, the country has a road map for building a rights-based society. The initiatives and efforts to make these rights a reality require a team effort. Individuals, organizations, governments, and international organizations have to cooperate. Together, they can create an ecosystem that strives for and promotes a better future.

Important events and benchmarks have marked Haiti's human rights journey. Even with the advent of the democratic era set off by the fall of the Duvalier regime on February 7, 1986, promoting and protecting human rights has been challenging. The 1987 constitution guarantees the rights to life, liberty, and security; freedom of expression; and the ban of torture and inhuman treatment. The constitution also established a system for protecting these rights, including an independent judiciary and the national ombudsman.

Though this Constitution is a landmark instrument for guaranteeing human rights, Haiti's path toward democracy and rule of law has not been smooth. The country has faced serious human rights issues. The terrible earthquake of 2010 worsened the challenges, causing widespread displacement, exorbitant loss of life, and extreme damage to infrastructure and services. International aid surged following the earthquake, but the slow recovery process has left many Haitians still living in precarious conditions.

Further political unrest remains a major challenge. President Jovenel Moïse's murder in 2021 pushed Haiti into a new crisis, exacerbating tensions and showcasing the fragility of the democratic system. Frequent protests and disturbances have displayed the population's dissatisfaction with corruption, impunity, and inadequate basic services.

Human rights abuse, including violence carried out by both governmental and non-state entities, is pervasive. Police brutality, gender-based violence, attacks on journalists, and human rights activists still undermine public confidence and the rule of law.

Civil society groups, such as the National Human Rights

Defense Network (RNDDH) and the Haitian Women's Solidarity (SOFA), usually advocate social justice and human rights. They record abuses, help victims, and promote changes. These groups challenge state and non-state actors to protect human rights.

From 2004 to 2017, the United Nations Stabilization Mission in Haiti (MINUSTAH) sought to uphold human rights and restore order. Still, there have been allegations of abuse by peacekeepers. International NGOs and donor groups continue to support humanitarian initiatives, human rights, and capacity-building.

Learning from the past and striving for a better future are crucial to navigating Haiti's complex human rights situation. International and regional frameworks for human rights protection, civil society, and the international community offer significant instruments and support for this endeavor.

A culture that upholds human rights and dignity can help Haiti change its society and inspire its own people and the rest of the globe. The Haitian people can forge a future in which human rights are not only concepts but also actual realities, notwithstanding the difficulty of the undertaking.

The sanctity of life is central to the concept of human rights. It asserts that every human life has inherent value and deserves protection, respect, and dignity. It is based on the notion that all human lives, regardless of age, gender, race, or socioeconomic situation, have inherent value and should be protected.

Many international human rights instruments, such as the Universal Declaration of Human Rights (UDHR), sanction this principle. The UDHR states that "everyone has the right to life, liberty, and security of person.[59]"

However, violence and instability erode the protection of human life in Haïti. Criminal activity, gang violence, and political unrest have resulted in many fatalities and injuries, fostering a culture that frequently disregards the worth of human life. It is challenging to protect citizens from violence because of the

[59] "Universal Declaration of Human Rights | United Nations."

ineffective enforcement of the law and the impunity of offenders.

Maintaining the sanctity of life requires having access to healthcare. However, Haiti's healthcare system is overburdened and underfunded. In recent years, gangs have destroyed many healthcare facilities. Many people suffer and die needlessly as a result of their inability to receive basic medical care. Inadequate healthcare infrastructure makes it challenging to deliver prompt and efficient medical care, and maternal and newborn mortality rates are still high.

Economic hardship and poverty directly affect the sanctity of life. Basic necessities like food, clean water, and shelter are less accessible when poverty is widespread. A greater death rate is a result of malnutrition and substandard living conditions, especially for vulnerable groups like children and the elderly. The struggle for survival in such situations often leads to a devaluation of human life.

Political instability and corruption in Haiti have hindered the government's ability to uphold the sanctity of life. Frequent leadership changes, a lack of political will, and ineffective governance prevent the implementation of policies and programs that protect and promote human life. This instability also drives economic downturns and violence, harming the general welfare of the people.

Strengthening Haiti's law enforcement and judicial institutions is vital to preserving our country's dignity of life. This starts with improving law enforcement personnel's capacity building and training so they are knowledgeable about ethical standards and human rights. Accountability mechanisms are also crucial to holding law enforcement officials responsible for abuses or misconduct.

Envisioning a future in Haiti where the sanctity of life is upheld requires a collective commitment to addressing current challenges and implementing practical measures. In this envisioned Haiti, the streets are safe, and communities are free from the threat of violence, with law enforcement agencies operating with integrity and respect for human rights. Healthcare services are accessible to all, regardless of location or socio-economic status, with well-equipped hospitals and dedicated healthcare professionals. Moreover, poverty is significantly reduced, economic opportunities are available to everyone, and social safety nets protect the most vulnerable. The government is stable and effective, committed to upholding human rights and the rule of law, with strong, transparent, and accountable democratic institutions. Civil society organizations and communities actively promote and protect human rights, fostering a culture of respect for human life and dignity deeply ingrained in society's fabric, supported by ongoing education and advocacy efforts.

According to the World Bank, in 2020, "About 60% of Haiti's population, or 6.3 million people, remain poor and 24%, or 2.5 million people, extremely poor (HHS 2012), with poverty highest in rural areas." This pervasive poverty is both a cause and consequence of human rights violations, affecting nearly every aspect of life for the Haitian people.

The UN Office of the High Commissioner for Human Rights issued a report covering September 25, 2023, to February 29, 2024. This report states:

> *The number of people killed and injured due to gang violence significantly increased in 2023—4,451 killed and 1,668 injured. The number of victims skyrocketed in the first three months of 2024—1,554 killed and 826 injured up to 22 March.*
>
> *Gangs continued to use sexual violence to brutalize, punish, and control people. Women have been raped during gang attacks on neighborhoods, in many cases, after seeing their husbands killed in front of them. According to the report, some women are forced into exploitative sexual relations with gang members. In addition, the rape of hostages continues to be used to coerce families into paying ransoms. Sexual violence remains severely underreported and largely unpunished.*
>
> *Gangs continue to recruit and abuse children—boys and girls—*

who are unable to leave gangs' ranks for fear of retaliation, which, in some instances, has led to young gang members being killed for trying to escape. Daily life is also disrupted by restrictions imposed by gangs on the movement of people, goods and services.[60]

Other widespread human rights violations have marred lives, in particular in the Port-au-Prince area and the Artibonite department.

Like many other countries, Haiti has to follow a set of international and regional instruments that protect and support human rights. These frameworks provide guidelines and standards that help shape national legislation and policies. Key human rights instruments and bodies relevant to Haiti include the United Nations Universal Declaration of Human Rights (UDHR), the Inter-American Commission on Human Rights (IACHR), the American Convention on Human Rights and its protocol in the area of Economic, Social, and Cultural Rights ("Protocol of San Salvador"), as well as other critical treaties and conventions such as the International Covenant on Civil and Political Rights (ICCPR) and the International Covenant on Economic, Social and Cultural Rights (ICESCR).

Adopted by the General Assembly of the United Nations in 1948, the historic Universal Declaration of Human Rights (UDHR) outlines basic human rights that must be universally protected. It comprises thirty articles that provide a comprehensive overview of the rights and freedoms to which all individuals are entitled. These principles include:

Equality and Non-Discrimination: The UDHR asserts that all human beings are born free and equal in dignity and rights (Article 1). It prohibits discrimination of any kind, including race, color, sex, language, religion, political or other opinions, national or social origin, property, birth, or other status (Article 2).

[60] "A/HRC/57/41: Situation of Human Rights in Haiti - Interim Report of the United Nations High Commissioner for Human Rights - Advance Edited Version | OHCHR."

Right to Life, Liberty, and Security: Everyone has the right to life, liberty, and security of person (Article 3). This principle is fundamental to protecting individuals against arbitrary violence and deprivation of freedom.

Freedom from Slavery and Torture: The declaration explicitly prohibits slavery, the slave trade, and torture or cruel, inhuman, or degrading treatment or punishment (Articles 4 and 5).

Right to Fair Trial: The UDHR guarantees the right to an effective remedy by competent national tribunals for acts violating fundamental rights (Article 8) and the right to a fair and public hearing by an independent and impartial tribunal (Article 10).

Freedom of Thought, Conscience, and Religion: The declaration upholds the freedom of thought, conscience, and religion (Article 18).

Freedom of Opinion and Expression: Everyone has the right to freedom of opinion and expression (Article 19).

Right to Work, Education, and Participation: The UDHR also recognizes economic, social, and cultural rights, including the right to work, education, and participation in cultural life (Articles 23, 26, and 27).[61]

Haiti has integrated numerous UDHR principles into its national legislation; however, implementation is still lacking. Human rights advocates pursue efforts toward national laws consistent with international human rights standards.

The Organization of American States (OAS) is mandated to promote and protect human rights in the Americas, including through the Inter-American Commission on Human Rights (IACHR). Since its inception in 1959, the IACHR has played a critical role in monitoring human rights conditions, investigating violations, and providing recommendations to member states.

Monitoring and Reporting: Through public proceedings, on-site visits, and the publication of reports, the IACHR oversees the human rights situation in member countries. These reports

[61] "Universal Declaration of Human Rights | United Nations."

identify areas of concern, document violations, and offer suggestions for enhancing human rights protection.

Petition and Case System: The IACHR accepts petitions from individuals, organizations, and NGOs that allege human rights violations committed by a member State. The Commission examines these petitions and, if they are admissible, may refer them to the Inter-American Court of Human Rights (IACtHR). This system offers a critical pathway for redress if national mechanisms are ineffective.

Thematic Rapporteurships: The IACHR designates special rapporteurs to concentrate on particular human rights concerns, including the rights of women, migrants, Indigenous peoples, and freedom of expression. These rapporteurs advocate for improved protections within their respective mandates, conduct studies, and hold consultations.

The IACHR has actively engaged with human rights concerns in Haiti. Over the years, the Commission has visited Haiti numerous times, issued several reports, and provided the Haitian government with recommendations. The IACHR has identified several critical areas of concern, including the absence of effective judicial mechanisms, discrimination against marginalized groups, impunity, and political violence.

The Commission's work is particularly significant to Haiti, as national institutions frequently encounter difficulties in effectively addressing human rights violations. The IACHR serves as an external mechanism for accountability and helps address human rights concerns within the nation.

In 1966, the United Nations General Assembly adopted the International Covenant on Civil and Political Rights (ICCPR), a critical international treaty delineating various civil and political rights.

The ICCPR is legally obligatory on its signatories, binding them to respect and guarantee these rights for all individuals within their jurisdiction.

Haiti ratified the ICCPR in 1991, pledging to uphold the civil and political rights the treaty enshrines. Nevertheless, obstacles continue to impede the full realization of these rights, including arbitrary detention, police brutality, restrictions on freedom of expression, and a lack of judicial independence. The ICCPR establishes a framework for promoting and strengthening civil and political rights through advocacy and reform initiatives.

Further, the United Nations General Assembly adopted another cornerstone instrument in 1966, the International Covenant on Economic, Social, and Cultural Rights (ICESCR), which focuses on the economic, social, and cultural rights indispensable for individuals' dignity and well-being.

Haiti ratified the ICESCR in 2013, reaffirming its commitment to economic, social, and cultural rights. Nevertheless, the country struggles to implement these rights due to pervasive poverty, inadequate infrastructure, and limited resources. The ICESCR provides a crucial framework for addressing these issues, guiding efforts to improve living conditions and access to Haiti's healthcare, education, and social services.

Haiti can strengthen its human rights framework and address its pressing challenges by enforcing its national legislation, aligning it with these international standards. Political will and pragmatic policies can bring about a society of respect for the dignity of life and human rights, ensuring that every Haitian enjoys the fundamental rights to which they are entitled.

A changed and fair Haiti is not a far-off dream but a realistic ambition. Haitians can create a country where every person's rights are respected and protected. They can proceed with optimism and commitment, knowing that by defending human rights, they lay the foundation for a better, more peaceful, and prosperous future.

CHAPTER 11

A CASE FOR EDUCATION AND ERADICATION OF ILLITERACY

Education is the most powerful weapon which you can use to change the world. Nelson Mandela, former President of South Africa

When I was a young boy in elementary school, life in Haiti had its own rhythm. The school day was split into two: mornings from 8:00 to 11:00 and afternoons from 2:00 to 4:00. During the midday break, a small group of boys, including Desruisseaux and four others, would come to my mom's house for a brief rest. From Pont Benoit, they walked each day for around one hour to reach the National School Louis Lamartiniere by 8:00 a.m., their laughter and conversation resounding down the dusty roads. Driven by a fire in their souls, they would make the same long walk back in the evening with exhausted legs but resolved to transcend the hand life had given them.

These boys came from vulnerable families, but they strongly desired to learn as though knowledge were the key to opening doors to a different future. It was about daring to dream beyond their village, where poverty appeared to span the horizon. With every stride they made and every day they spent in their classrooms, they battled the weight of generations and resolved to change their lives and those of their families.

Years later, Desruisseaux arrived in the United States and demonstrated that the trials and tribulations had been well worth it by forging a successful career path. The other four boys have become pillars for their families, using the education they had fought for to lift their loved ones toward a better life. The dusty roads they once traveled on as children had led them to places where they could be trailblazers for many in their families.

This story is not unique; it reflects the experience of many children who have overcome challenges to get an education for a better future. Education is not merely a means to achieve personal success; it is the cornerstone of social transformation and national development. Education nurtures hope. It is the key to unlocking the nation's potential and fostering economic growth and social cohesion.

The impact of education on social transformation is profound. The case for education in Haiti is a plea to invest in the minds and dreams of Haiti's children to empower future generations to lead, innovate, and transform their nation. Through education, Haiti can rise above its challenges and chart a course toward a prosperous and harmonious future.

Haiti's educational history is deeply intertwined with its colonial past. During the colonial era, education was a privilege reserved for the elite, primarily the children of French settlers. The education system was designed to serve the colonial administration, with a curriculum focused on European ideals and values, banning enslaved Africans from formal education.

The Haitian Revolution, culminating in the country's independence in 1804, brought significant changes and new challenges. Building an education system from the ground up was a monumental undertaking for the newly established republic. Independent Haiti's leaders acknowledged the significance of education in the context of national development and social cohesion. Nevertheless, the economic hardships and the enduring effects of colonial exploitation posed a challenge in developing a comprehensive and inclusive educational infrastructure.

Throughout the nineteenth and early twentieth centuries,

several governments endeavored to reform the education system to improve the quality of and access to education. Nevertheless, these initiatives were frequently stifled. Political instability has been a persistent challenge, as frequent changes in government have disrupted educational policies and reforms. Economic constraints have also been a significant factor, restricting the government's capacity to invest in infrastructure, teacher training, and learning materials.

Despite these obstacles, there have been periods of significant progress. In the mid-twentieth century, the government made a concerted effort to increase the availability of primary education. New teacher training schools and curricula were steps toward improving the quality of education. International organizations and NGOs also began to play a more prominent role in supporting educational initiatives.

The 2010 earthquake dealt a devastating blow to Haiti's education system, destroying hundreds of schools and disrupting the education of millions of children. Foreign aid and local initiatives helped rebuild and improve the educational infrastructure during the post-earthquake reconstruction process. In recent years, we have seen an increasing understanding of the need for substantial educational reform.

The government and stakeholders aim to create a more inclusive and fair education system. Initiatives to improve teacher training, integrate technology in schools, and expand vocational training programs are positive advances.

Recent data shows Haiti's literacy rate is around 61%, lower than the norm of 90% in Latin America and the Caribbean. The primary school enrollment rate is approximately 88 percent. However, at the secondary level, only about 20% of youngsters attend high school[62]. Many pupils do not complete elementary school, resulting in poor educational attainment. These data highlight the critical need for systemic adjustments to help more

[62] "Education in Haiti."

Haitian children pursue and complete their education.

Education, especially literacy and numeracy, is a powerful catalyst for personal fulfillment and the enjoyment of human rights. Citizens living in a democratic system need to know how to read and write to understand the scope and limits of their rights and duties.

Literacy is essential for individuals to exercise other rights and for countries to mitigate situations of vulnerability and achieve many of the Sustainable Development Goals, including eradicating poverty, reducing inequalities, promoting economic growth, and strengthening peace, justice, and institutions. Professor Carl Sagan rightly said, *"Frederick Douglass taught that literacy is the path from slavery to freedom. There are many types of slavery and many freedoms, but reading is always the way.*[63]*"* The former director-general of UNESCO, Irina Bokova, said:

> *"Literacy is much more than an educational priority—it is the ultimate investment in the future and the first step towards all the new forms of literacy required in the twenty-first century.*[64]*"*

Everyday experience shows how literacy is a cornerstone. Many countries require passengers to complete immigration and customs forms before entry. Illiterate passengers must seek assistance and rely on the kindness of others to complete these forms. This scene demonstrates the challenges that illiterate individuals have in breaking the cycle of dependence. They also face challenges in communicating effectively and expressing a range of life experiences. With a limited understanding of their rights and duties, they are often exploited. Their limitations also cause them to rely excessively on their emotions, personal predispositions, and cultural prejudices.

Literacy rates in Latin America and the Caribbean vary

---

[63] Sagan, The Demon-Haunted World.

[64] "Message from Ms Irina Bokova, Director-General of UNESCO, on the Occasion of International Literacy Day: Literacies for the 21st Century, 8 September 2013 - UNESCO Digital Library."

significantly, with some countries faring better than others. The Economic Commission for Latin America and the Caribbean (ECLAC) states, "Despite the important advances of recent decades in the educational coverage and literacy rate of the population of Latin America and the Caribbean, illiteracy in the adult population, especially that has been called functional, it continues to be a present problem and a reflection of inequality in the region. A sample of the size of this is that there is still, on average, 9% of the population aged 15 years and over in the countries of Latin America and the Caribbean in a condition of absolute illiteracy. If this is considered from a functional perspective – such as the set of skills and competencies required to function in people's life contexts – this figure would grow significantly."[65]

According to the World Population Review, the highest literacy rates in the region are in Cuba (99.7 percent), Argentina (99 percent), Chile (97 percent), and Uruguay (98.8 percent). However, the lowest literacy rates include countries such as Haiti (61.7 percent), Nicaragua (83 percent) and Guatemala (84 percent)[66].

The inability to read and write limits participation in social, political, and economic life, thus hindering the enjoyment of several other rights. Examples of the impact of illiteracy on the enjoyment of other rights include:

Right to work: Illiteracy limits people's ability to access better employment opportunities, which reduces their earning potential and limits their ability to contribute to the well-being of their families.

Right to health: Illiteracy limits individuals' ability to access health information, understand medical instructions, and communicate effectively with healthcare providers. This restriction can lead to a lack of access to health services.

[65] Roldán and Gálvez, "La alfabetización de personas jóvenes y adultas en América Latina y el Caribe: análisis de los principales programas."
[66] "Literacy Rate by Country 2024."

Right to participate in democratic processes: Illiteracy limits individuals' ability to participate fully in democratic processes, such as voting and access to information on public policies. This constraint also limits participation in decision-making processes.

Right to access justice: Illiteracy limits individuals' ability to access justice. They may have difficulty understanding legal documents or communicating effectively with lawyers and judges. This barrier can lead to a lack of access to justice and violations of their rights.

Cuba has succeeded in a literacy campaign using effective strategies. First, the government led the campaign, which provided the necessary resources and support to ensure its success. Second, the campaign mobilized many volunteers motivated to improve their communities and contribute to the country's development. Finally, the campaign used innovative and effective teaching methods, such as the Yo sí puedo method, designed to be accessible and effective for adult learners. Several other Latin American and Caribbean countries have had good experiences combating illiteracy. Here are a few examples:

Venezuela: The Bolivarian Literacy Campaign, launched in 2003, has reduced the country's illiteracy rate from 7.2 percent to 1.3 percent in just one year. The campaign used various strategies, including community educators and the promotion of reading circles.[67]

Nicaragua: In 1980, the Sandinista administration initiated a literacy drive, reducing the country's illiteracy rate from 50% to 13%. The campaign used volunteers, creative teaching methods, and community involvement.

Bolivia's Yo sí puedo initiative, begun in 2008, lowered the country's illiteracy rate from 14% to 3.8% within three years. The campaign used radio and television programs, community involvement, and multicultural and multilingual education.

Ecuador's Together We Learn More campaign, begun in 2008,

[67] venezueladmin, "Venezuela and Bolivia Celebrate Beating Illiteracy."

has reduced illiteracy from 7.2% to 3.3% in under three years. The campaign involved community educators, promoted intercultural and bilingual education, and implemented innovative teaching methods.[68]

These campaigns inspire how illiteracy can be effectively eradicated, even under challenging circumstances.

Haiti's frequent protean crises reveal serious shortcomings in the education sector regarding the imbalance between demand and supply and content relevance. According to UNESCO, almost 38% of the population aged 15-65 was illiterate in 2022[69]. To address the long-standing issue of illiteracy in Haiti, literacy and numeracy for all citizens is a must, as individual mental growth precedes collective progress.

Universal literacy is vital to the country's survival and progress and cannot be confined to the government's prerogative. Every citizen must mobilize energy, resources, and goodwill to contribute to the eradication of illiteracy in every sector, especially the private sector and civil society.

Is literacy a priority at a time when Haiti is facing one of its worst political, social, economic, and security crises? The response is that the best time to pursue universal literacy was after independence in 1804; the second-best time is now. Every day that passes with a large number of compatriots in intellectual darkness and mental dormancy is a period when Haiti sows the seed of poverty and violence.

When it comes to violence and insecurity, we need literacy to understand Martin Luther King Jr.'s words: "*Nonviolence means avoiding not only outward physical violence but also inward violence of the mind. Not only do you refuse to shoot a man, but you refuse to hate him. . . . We adopt the means of nonviolence because our goal is a community at peace with itself. We will try to persuade with our words, but if our words fail, we*

[68] "Basic Education for Young People and Adults, Ecuador - Effective Literacy and Numeracy Practices Database – LitBase."
[69] "Gal_country_profiles_haiti.Pdf."

will try to persuade with our actions."

To achieve universal literacy, leaders from different sectors, especially the government, must exercise their responsibility to lead the way by developing and displaying a burning desire and an iron will. Napoleon Hill rightly says: "The starting point of all realization is desire." In other words, a burning desire is a must to achieve desired results.

The availability of technology and learning material is a necessary but not sufficient condition. A permanent, all-out campaign to promote literacy is essential. This campaign will motivate potential beneficiaries to exercise their right to education and keep the flame of wise governance burning among policymakers and influencers by prioritizing literacy. This campaign and its outcome have enormous benefits, including:

The exercise by the government of its role as a political agenda-builder. By taking back control through an incessant discourse of glorification or sublimation of education and literacy, the nation's leaders will divert attention from cultural shortcomings and disastrous news to bring it toward positive and legitimate aspirations.

The reduction of the phenomenon of idleness, especially among young people. Young volunteers with a good level of education will be able to support learners using their mobile phones or computers.

The redirection of energies toward an ambitious national project transcends political divisions, alternations, and particular interests.

The achievement of universal literacy and its corollary, functional literacy, will serve as the basis for rebuilding the nation, revitalizing institutions, and for the collective ownership of the lifelong learning process, social transformation, and economic takeoff.

Building a society on illiteracy is like building a beautiful house on shaky foundations. Thus, no stone should remain unturned until every child or citizen of our nation has access to literacy. A continuous literacy campaign will facilitate exercising all other rights and make democracy more stable, dynamic, and sustainable.

Personal development determines collective development. Therefore, every public policy should include a literacy or training dimension to achieve the desired results.

As former UN Secretary-General Kofi Annan pointed out:

> *Literacy is a bridge between misery and hope. It is a tool for everyday life in modern society. It is a bulwark against poverty and a building block of development, an essential complement to investments in roads, dams, clinics, and factories. Literacy is a platform for democratization and a vector for promoting cultural and national identity. Especially for girls and women, it is an agent of family health and nutrition. For everyone, everywhere, literacy is, along with education in general, a basic human right. Literacy is, finally, the road to human progress and the means through which every man, woman and child can realize his or her full potential.*[70]

The COVID-19 epidemic highlights the importance of technology in education worldwide, including Haiti. The pandemic caused school closures and disrupted traditional learning, leading to a quick shift to virtual learning. Despite challenges, the shift demonstrated technology's powerful role in improving education under any circumstances. Technology helped students continue their study through online platforms and virtual classrooms.

Using technology effectively in Haitian education requires following best practices, increasing internet connectivity, and offering affordable digital devices. Customized e-learning solutions for the Haitian environment will improve learning and guarantee user-friendly interfaces and accessibility.

These platforms will include interactive lectures, videos, and tests to accommodate several learning styles. Teachers will have to

[70] "SECRETARY-GENERAL STRESSES NEED FOR POLITICAL WILL AND RESOURCES TO MEET CHALLENGE OF FIGHT AGAINST ILLITERACY | Meetings Coverage and Press Releases."

acquire digital skills to enhance the learning experience. Updated school materials in Creole and French will help increase relevance and efficiency.

Blending the conventional classroom with the online platform will enhance the advantages of both methods. This model is especially useful in areas with limited access to technology.

Traditional and social media, alongside digital platforms, can effectively support education and training in Haiti. Students in remote regions with inadequate internet connectivity may benefit from educational radio and television programs.

Mobile phones are ubiquitous in Haiti. Interactive voice response (IVR) systems and SMS-based learning can provide students with educational content and assessments. These techniques are cost-effective and capable of reaching a broad audience. YouTube, WhatsApp, and Facebook are examples of social media platforms that can facilitate communication between students and teachers and disseminate educational content. Among the ways to use social media include distributing lesson videos, organizing live Q&A sessions, and creating study groups. Digital tools housed in community centers will assist students lacking home access to technology. These venues offer online learning, internet access, and computer literacy courses.

Rwanda's educational achievements show how transforming technology can be for learning. Early in the 2000s, this country struggled with low literacy rates and inadequate infrastructure, among other issues. The government launched aggressive initiatives to incorporate technology into schools, revolutionizing education.

Aiming to promote digital literacy and interactive learning by giving elementary school children laptops, One Laptop Per Child was a key priority for Rwanda.

The government launched ambitious projects to transform education by integrating technology into classrooms. The One Laptop Per Child program provides computers to primary school pupils to promote digital literacy and interactive learning. The government has invested in internet connectivity to guarantee that remote schools can access online resources.

Teacher training is another crucial element of the program. The government offers professional development initiatives to enable teachers to use technology effectively. These strategies raise student involvement and improve education quality.

Bangladesh exemplifies how new technologies can overcome educational challenges. This country utilized mobile technology to tackle high attrition rates and restricted access to schooling in rural areas. The Mobile Education for Hard-to-Reach Areas initiative used mobile phones to deliver educative content to children in remote locations.

Students could complete assessments and receive instruction via mobile phone through SMS-based lessons and interactive voice response (IVR). This method effectively reached females and children from low-income families who may have otherwise missed out on formal education. Bangladesh also implemented the BRAC Education Program, establishing informal institutions in rural areas. These schools used locally devised curricula and hired community members as teachers to provide culturally relevant and accessible education.

Strategic public-private collaborations have significantly improved India's education scene. Pratham's Read India campaign sought to raise literacy rates among elementary school pupils using creative teaching strategies and community involvement. Pratham mainly focused on giving children strong reading and math skills through learning camps. Held over school holidays, these camps applied interactive and activity-based learning strategies to make education more engaging. Pratham created digital learning tools like videos and smartphone apps to improve learning. These technologies guarantee affordable access for students from underprivileged backgrounds.

Kenya has made notable educational advancements by focusing on teacher skill improvement. Understanding the need for excellent pedagogy for student success, the government increased the number of teachers, trained them, and stimulated professional development. The Teacher Service Commission (TSC) mandated teachers apply student-centered teaching approaches.

TSC has used technology to assess teacher effectiveness and offer feedback for skill improvement, helping teachers stay on their toes. Kenya started the Digital Literacy Program to incorporate technology into basic education. By equipping schools with digital devices and training teachers to use them, the program sought to improve learning efficiency and prepare the pupils for a digital future.

Examples from Rwanda, Bangladesh, India, and Kenya illustrate that underprivileged areas can accomplish notable educational development despite hardship. These countries have successfully imparted quality education, created public-private alliances, and used technology. These projects can inspire Haiti to build a more inclusive, strong, and successful educational system enabling every pupil to realize their full potential.

Haiti's pathway toward development and prosperity depends on education. The nation must improve its infrastructure, educational materials, and teacher credentials to achieve long-term results. The transforming power of education is immeasurable. Nonetheless, much-needed education reforms depend on political will and citizen support via direct involvement, funding, and advocacy. Civil society organizations can also help improve education by advocating for laws prioritizing education and raising awareness of the threats to the educational system.

Education serves as the cornerstone of a promising future. By investing in the minds and dreams of Haiti's children, we are investing in the nation's capacity to overcome its challenges. Haitians can unite to advocate for Haiti's transformation and establish a legacy of optimism, opportunity, and progress for future generations. Haiti can pledge its unwavering commitment to this cause, confident in its ability to transform lives and create a brighter future through education.

Education mitigates the risks that orality poses. Haiti has been a society where orality, verbal transmission of information, and informal communication prevail over written records. Oral traditions support the preservation of moral precepts, historical narratives, and social customs. While orality strengthens social ties, it challenges governance, economic growth, and administration.

The public administration relies heavily on oral instructions and undocumented decisions, leading to inefficiencies and an institutional memory deficit. Due to a lack of reliable records, government offices face difficulty upholding accountability and policy continuity. Political transitions cause disruptions, as past governments' oral agreements are typically ignored due to the lack of a formal record. An orality culture may be conducive to misinformation and manipulation.

Informal agreements and transactions raise the possibility of fraud, lawsuits, insufficient legal and financial protection. Businesses and people will struggle to defend their rights without written agreements, which reduces investment and causes less economic stability.

Education will empower Haiti to navigate the development maze and illuminate paths that circumvent pitfalls. Education is Haiti's best and most profitable investment in achieving transformation.

CHAPTER 12

CRAFTING A NEW NARRATIVE IN HAITI

Whoever would love life and see good days must keep their tongue from evil and their lips from deceitful speech. 1 Peter 3:10

Speech has power. Words do not fade. What starts out as a sound ends in a deed.[71] *Abraham Joshua Heschel, theologian and philosopher*

Haiti has experienced resilience and hopelessness. Stories of triumph and tragedy dance a complex choreography that shapes the collective consciousness. Often stalking the nation, a web of challenges has cast a long shadow on its past achievements. Crippling poverty and terrible natural and man-made disasters—have challenged resilience.

The persistent nagging poverty narrative has negatively impacted Haiti's social and economic development, sustaining a cycle of suffering. This narrative clouds Haiti's potential by eclipsing its people's genius and culture's brilliance. Likewise, the political system has seen many coups, transitions, and contested elections that have left the Haitian people with a sense of disenfranchisement and helplessness. The narrative that has fractured the efforts to effect meaningful change has fueled stagnation and stifled progress.

[71] richardsh, "7 December 1965 Rabbi Abraham Joshua Heschel alongside Martin Luther King #otdimjh."

Nevertheless, Haiti must confront the devitalizing narratives to usher in a new era of progress and prosperity. This determination is essential for Haiti to realize its full potential and regain its place on the world stage. Author Edwidge Danticat said, *"I think there's something really beautiful about embracing who you are and owning and accepting all of you and knowing that everything about you is purposeful.*[72]*"*

The purpose of Haiti's existence under the sun must be understood and embraced in order to create narratives that unite and inspire Haitians to build a Haiti where hope is as radiant as the sun on its golden shores. The primary objective of a new narrative is to transform minds and souls rather than merely alter words. Haitians can rewrite their story by deconstructing limiting beliefs, adopting a positive mindset, and implementing practical strategies for change.

Storytelling has been a fundamental component of human culture, influencing our perceptions, beliefs, and actions, from ancient mythologies and legends to contemporary literature and media.

In Haiti, stories unite individuals from various generations and communities, safeguarding their history, culture, and identity. Stories are vital from literature to gastronomy, from traditional medicine to popular celebrations. They promote awareness, values, and perseverance. They profoundly impact society, shaping our perspective of ourselves, and the world. Walter Fisher, the esteemed cultural critic, once observed, *"Human beings are storytelling animals.*[73]*"* Our identities, desires, and actions are shaped by the tales we tell ourselves and believe.

Haitians' perceptions of themselves and their place in the world derive from stories, ranging from the triumphant narrative of the Haitian Revolution to the prevalent stories of resignation and defeatism. The stories we choose to tell and the stories we

---

[72] Danticat, We're Alone.

[73] Fisher, Human Communication as Narration.

believe define our lives, influencing our identities, aspirations, and actions. A negative narrative affects self-esteem, undermines confidence, and spoils the implementation of significant change.

Moreover, narratives can be instruments of oppression and control, influencing perceptions of injustice, privilege, and power. Haiti is still struggling with the legacy of colonialism and imperialism. The narrative of foreign interventions has fueled distrust and resentment toward external powers, perpetuating a sense of victimhood and dependency. However, the country has yet to experience inspiring stories of good governance and uplifting leadership as society oscillates between authoritarianism and anarchy.

However, narratives are not static or unchanging; they are dynamic and fluid, capable of altering over time in response to changing circumstances and perspectives. The mind can be a fertile nursery for ideas or a violent battleground. The struggle to control the narrative is often a battle for hearts and minds, with far-reaching implications for Haiti's future.

Narratives can cause Haiti to move to the top of the mountain of stability and well-being or keep the country on the slippery slope of political and social neglect and unrest. Black nationalist and leader of the Pan-Africanist movement Marcus Garvey said, *"The man who is not able to develop and use his mind is bound to be the slave of the other man who uses his mind."*[74] The transformative potential of storytelling can prepare Haitians to harness the power of their minds for the greater good of Haiti.

It's time to construct a fresh narrative that embraces the boundless opportunities the future holds and transcends past limitations. Creating this fresh narrative requires bravery, creativity, and collaboration. But where ought we to start? When will we call a better peace and prosperity into existence?

The vision and energy from Haiti's history can inspire triumphs and achievements in every walk of life. Dwelling on or

[74] "The African Nova Scotian Roots of Bob Marley's 'Redemption Song.'"

reliving past success should not lead to a backward-looking philosophy or navel-gazing attitude, for the moments of grandeur have preceded extended periods in the wilderness of daze and perplexity.

Learning from previous mistakes while addressing present challenges can help Haiti to build a desirable future. Artists, singers, authors, and storytellers will hone and magnify Haiti's voice as the narrative changes, challenging preconceptions. A fresh narrative can help generate financial opportunities, support small businesses, alleviate poverty, and advance long-term development.

Sharing inspirational stories helps unlock Haiti's potential by encouraging self-development and equipping future generations with the knowledge and skills they need to thrive in a changing world. A fresh optimistic narrative will focus on a better educational system that advances creativity, critical thinking, and lifelong learning. The widespread adoption of technology will create fresh opportunities for economic development and social improvement. With telemedicine, renewable energy, mobile banking, and e-commerce, technology will change communities and individuals.

Thanks to servant leadership, Haiti's fresh perspective will sustain civic virtue, fostering principles of accountability, tolerance, and respect of human rights—hence, a new culture of democracy and pluralism establishing the groundwork for a more fair and equitable society.

Crafting an inspirational narrative for Haiti is a journey of hope, excitement, and endless possibilities. Haitian poet and politician Jacques Roumain is believed to have said, "Open your eyes and see the image of your own liberation". Understanding the power of narrative might help Haiti to become peaceful and prosperous.

Often referred to as "konplo," conspiracy theories show how political discourse can be weaponized. Political culture abounds in these theories. By blaming political rivals and foreign intervention, leaders generate uncertainty and dodge accountability, erode confidence in democratic institutions.

The emergence of grassroots movements and civil society organizations striving to promote transparency and accountability in government and hold politicians accountable is a hopeful sign of progress. These movements, which range from youth-led initiatives to anti-corruption activists, serve as a source of optimism in Haiti's pursuit of social justice and political stability.

Political leaders' rhetoric is a powerful force that can inspire or incite, unite or divide. Haitians must confront divisive discourse, foster dialogue and healing, and strive for a future where politics prioritizes the common good over individual interests.

Countless limiting beliefs have become entrenched in the narrative over the years, standing in the way of progress. Finding and fixing them offers an Ariane's thread guiding out of the maze of stagnation or deterioration. Among the most often used and destructive concepts in Haiti is the victim mentality. It reinforces the view that foreign forces mainly cause domestic problems.

Notwithstanding this indisputable truth, keeping a victim mindset limits individual and social development. This limitation results in a cycle of dependence and inaction whereby people rely on external assistance rather than spearheading internal transformation. The victim mindset affects Haitians' agency by implying that they cannot shape their own future.

Changing this attitude calls for an empowering culture. Through imagination, determination, and success stories, Haitians will view themselves as active agents of change rather than helpless victim of circumstances. Community projects encouraging civic participation, entrepreneurship, and leadership will enable people to live up to their potential and change their neighborhoods.

The victim mindset begets the second limiting belief, a scarcity mindset. Most Haitians believe that deprivation is inevitable. This kind of thinking resists efforts at economic growth and development, lessens confidence and ambition, and leads people to think their situation is a fatality. Emphasizing the success stories of Haitians who have surmounted financial obstacles through creativity and entrepreneurship can help tackle this limited belief. The success stories will help people to believe in themselves and break the cycle of poverty.

Still another limiting viewpoint is that political instability and corruption are unavoidable. This idea suggests that the results will remain the same regardless of the person in charge, fostering cynicism, widespread apathy, and political disengagement. To challenge this assumption, it is imperative to support civic education and active participation in the political process.

By sensitizing people on their rights and duties, grassroots movements and community organizations can help individuals hold their leaders accountable. For instance, the youth-led movement Nou Pap Dòmi (We Will Not Sleep) from Haiti has successfully mobilized young people to demand transparency and good governance. These initiatives can inspire a younger generation of Haitians to believe in their capacity to shape the destiny of their nation by offering specific instances of how active civic participation can bring about favorable results.

Moreover, Haiti's sensitivity to natural disasters has led to a fatalistic perspective that says little can be done to mitigate their impact. This view sometimes results in lethargy and resignation, hindering proactive steps to improve disaster resilience and preparedness. Awareness, adapted infrastructure, and funding are necessary to change this narrative and strengthen disaster readiness. For example, early warning systems and the design of anti-seismic buildings will help prevent deaths and reduce economic losses. Resilient infrastructure and community-based training programs that impart practical skills for emergency response can substantially mitigate the effects of natural disasters and debunk this limiting belief.

In Haitian culture, superstition is a profoundly ingrained and detrimental belief that undermines personal responsibility and self-development. Though traditional beliefs and cultural practices help to create a sense of connection and identity, superstition usually results in fear and resignation. It can lead to a fatalistic viewpoint whereby people credit supernatural powers alone—rather than their own actions—for their achievements or failures.

This mindset undermines personal agency, discourages proactive efforts to improve one's circumstances, erodes values, and debilitates the national psyche. These issues undermine personal integrity and accountability. Hence resignation, complacency, or indifference.

Spiritual limbo has overwhelmed the Haitian culture for more than two centuries, flowing from contradicting life philosophies. Professing to be Christians in the morning and practicing voodoo at night has placed most people on the fence on vital issues. This unholy mixture has created confusion in the minds of many Haitians, leading to an opportunistic attitude toward life. This spiritual limbo has fostered a debilitating attitude, weakened the sense of responsibility, and generated pervasive superstition. Mistrust and anxiety result from such an attitude, which stifles integrity.

Democracy and civilized societies consider freedom of faith to be a sacred principle. There is no reason for anyone to interfere with an individual's personal expression of faith.

However, being definite in what god(s) one believes in matters, as it ensures clarity of mind and determines the principles guiding one's life. Preaching love for the neighbor in the morning and scaring her with mystical dealings at night is not an attitude that feeds social harmony, order, and the pursuit of prosperity and happiness.

The nation-building process focuses on replacing fear with faith and confidence. Fear has hindered progress and dominated Haiti's social and political environment for too long. Fear can be devastating and paralyzing. Fear is insidious, debilitating, and paralyzing. Franklin D. Roosevelt's famous words during the Great Depression, *"The only thing we have to fear is fear itself*[75]*,"* resonate here. Haiti must cultivate awareness of faith and trust if she hopes to build a brighter future.

Fear has perpetuated an underlying culture of violence. Conversely, trust fosters social harmony, progress, and nonviolence. The nation-building process should be sustained by the principle of nonviolence, which should be deeply ingrained in a new narrative and a revitalized Haitian culture. A consistent awareness campaign could help prepare people to absorb and use this new mindset and fresh approach to life and thinking. Haiti may see enduring peace, security, justice, and universal education by purposefully and relentlessly pursuing these goals.

Unlocking Haiti's potential and building a peaceful and prosperous future depend on identifying and transforming these limiting beliefs. A society that values proactive participation, personal growth, and resilience can help overcome challenges from the past. However, some cultural practices and social norms can support restrictive ideas, extending inequality and exclusion cycles.

Critical thinking will help evaluate how the limiting beliefs affect society. A transformed mindset will drive development and lead to a reborn Haiti. An entirely new narrative will profoundly impact Haiti's self-image and future. The new narrative will improve chances that the Haitian people will live up to the grandeur of their revolution. Haiti must be a nation that values its history, appreciates the present, and conquers the future.

[75] "'Only Thing We Have to Fear Is Fear Itself': FDR's First Inaugural Address."

CHAPTER 13

ERADICATING POVERTY AND CREATING WEALTH

Overcoming poverty is not a task of charity; it is an act of justice. Like Slavery and Apartheid, poverty is not natural. It is man-made, and it can be overcome and eradicated by the actions of human beings. Nelson Mandela, former president of South Africa

Haiti is at a critical juncture. It is tasked with eradicating poverty and establishing pathways to generate enduring wealth. This challenge is not unique to the country; it is a global ambition encapsulated in the United Nations' Sustainable Development Goal 1 (SDG 1): "End poverty in all its forms everywhere.[76]" Although the journey to end poverty carries its complexities, Haitian leaders can offer a roadmap that addresses the root causes of poverty while laying the foundation for a culture of wealth generation and prosperity.

It is simplistic to understand poverty in Haiti merely from an income standpoint. The issue encompasses social exclusion, inadequate infrastructure, low education levels, and limited access to healthcare. For many Haitians, poverty is a lack of both financial resources and opportunities for a dignified and fulfilling life. Since poverty is often intergenerational, every new baby is likely to live a life with the same challenges as their parents. Breaking the cycle of poverty calls for a careful review of the policies and ideologies

[76] dpicampaigns, "Goal 1."

sustaining it.

The potential for prosperity is as present as for poverty. Prosperity transcends material possessions. It calls for an abundance attitude, entrepreneurship, and developed human capital. Haiti's development requires everyone, particularly the society leaders, to see themselves leaving poverty and helping to create shared prosperity. A paradigm change is necessary to reach this objective of empowering people and communities to generate wealth via creativity, collaboration, and shared responsibility.

Wealth creation and poverty elimination work side by side. Initiatives to reduce poverty also lay the foundation for long-term prosperity. By tackling poverty holistically—that is, with regard to health, education, governance, housing and economic inclusion—Haiti can reach SDG 1. Implementing creative ideas, developing a wealth-generating mindset, and leveraging international cooperation lead to a transformed Haiti.

Effective legislation and cultural changes can break the cycle of poverty and promote a mindset of wealth generation. Achieving the aim of poverty eradication and wealth development requires strategic planning, creative thinking, and collective will. Haiti has the potential to overcome insurmountable challenges to reduce poverty and build a wealth-oriented culture.

Poverty is not solely defined by income or economic productivity; it is a state of deprivation that affects many aspects of life. Developed by OPHI and the UN Development Program (UNDP) for inclusion in UNDP's Human Development Reports, the Multidimensional Poverty Index (MPI) acknowledges poverty as a multidimensional phenomenon, including deprivations in health, education, and living conditions. This Index offers a more realistic picture of Haiti's challenges as well as a valuable framework for handling them.

Health is a critical dimension of poverty. Lack of access to necessary healthcare services results in untreated diseases, low life expectancy, and a cycle of illness that reduces productivity and learning capability. Maternal and child mortality rates remain high, and the healthcare system fails to meet the needs of the population. Poor health has personal and economic costs, since a sick workforce reduces production.

Education is a key component of multidimensional poverty. Haitians in rural areas face restricted access to quality education due to the scarcity and dispersion of institutions, inadequate materials and underpaid teachers. As a result, many pupils struggle to develop the skills needed to transcend poverty.

The cycle of poverty persists in the absence of education, as each generation inherits the same constraints as the previous one. Quality and relevance must be top priorities to break this cycle and expand educational facilities, so young Haitians must be equipped with the mental tools they need to navigate the modern world.

The low standard of living reflects and exacerbates the poverty situation. Many Haitians lack access to safe housing, adequate sanitation, and clean water. Subsistence farming is common in rural areas, yet productivity remains poor without modern tools or techniques. Urban slums are caused by overcrowding and poor infrastructure, with limited prospects for reform. Material hardship thwarts effective planning for the future because of an everyday fight for survival. Particularly for vulnerable populations like women, children in rural areas, social exclusion aggravates existing challenges.

To end poverty, Haiti must not only solve material deprivations but also the political, social, and structural inequalities that support the marginalization of the masses.

The multidimensional approach to understanding poverty shows that tackling poverty requires more than boosting incomes or offering short-term aid. It demands an integrated strategy that addresses the full spectrum of deprivation. Poverty in Haiti is not simply a byproduct of unfortunate circumstances; it is perpetuated by entrenched practices and systemic barriers that limit progress. These forces have to be removed to chart a course for sustainable development.

Some traditions and systems generate poverty and prevent many people from escaping it. Historically, an unfair economic structure has benefited a select few at the detriment of the underprivileged many.

Corruption affects all levels of government and business, diverting resources intended for the common good to the powerful elite. This system exacerbates wealth disparity and undermines trust in institutions, hindering citizens' productive participation in society. When citizens lose confidence in their government's ability to manage resources fairly and efficiently, they feel detached, disempowered, and disheartened. Inequity in Haiti leads to poverty for millions with limited prospects for advancement.

Dependence on foreign aid fuels poverty rather than stimulating prosperity. While humanitarian assistance is necessary during crises, it might create dependency rather than empowerment over time. Aid can provide immediate relief in emergency situations, but it does not address the root causes of poverty. Distracting people from self-sustaining economic activity and heavy dependence on foreign aid can damage local projects and stifle innovation. Haiti has to stop depending on foreign help and start investing in the abilities of its people so that people may take charge of their financial fate and abolish poverty.

Negative cultural attitudes sustain poverty, enabling survival to take front stage rather than growth. Volatility and unrest have resulted in a tendency to give immediate needs top priority over long-term development. This reactive attitude stifles investments in business, education, and future-oriented projects that can create long-term wealth.

Clientelism—exchanging favors for political support—worsens inequity and inefficiency, impeding social and economic development. It prioritizes political allegiance over innovation and merit-based advancement.

Another significant stumbling block to development is land ownership and agricultural inefficiencies. Although agriculture is a substantial source of income for Haiti, many farmers do not own their property. This lack of ownership restricts their ability to invest in innovation and increase productivity. Outdated farming techniques and a lack of innovative technologies result in low agricultural output, food insecurity, and limited economic opportunities. Haiti can go from subsistence farming to sustainable livelihoods by making technological investments and agrarian reform.

Constant and self-reinforcing poverty derives from economic disparity, low education, poor healthcare, external dependency, and dysfunctional institutional systems. If Haiti is to break the cycle, it must solve the underlying causes of poverty and provide an environment that gives its people tools and chances for long-term development. A wealth-generating culture and an empowered mindset will transform deeply ingrained habits and result in a fair future.

Central to this shift is the power of faith and hope. For too long, many Haitians have been conditioned to see their circumstances as shaped by a long history of colonialism, political instability, and natural disasters. This belief induces a sense of resignation, in which individuals prioritize survival over pursuing more substantial opportunities. People must realize the need for change and their power to determine their fate if the country is to generate prosperity. Determination to pursue long-term objectives despite challenges will bring about change.

Entrepreneurship is an effective strategy for cultivating a success mentality. It is the process of spotting opportunities where others see obstacles. Risk-taking and creative people have the power to transform local businesses and communities. They can unleash their underused potential in many areas, including agriculture, tourism, crafts, and technology.

Implanting the entrepreneurship culture calls for breaking

through obstacles using creativity to access resources. The entrepreneurial attitude will enable Haitians to realize their potential. Vocational training, financial support, and mentoring programs will empower people to launch companies, implement their ideas, and provide employment possibilities.

Similarly, entrepreneurs need access to market networks, investment opportunities, and credit, both locally and globally. Partnerships with overseas investors, community-based savings organizations, and microfinance efforts can help small firms become sustainable operations. In this manner, the opportunity to generate wealth is no longer limited to a select few, but becomes accessible to the general population.

In this sense, the ultimate objective is to move to a wealth-generating paradigm. Wealth includes access to social capital, healthcare, education, empowerment and agency, and financial means. Forward-looking policies have to solve the underlying causes of poverty and encourage innovation and expansion to eliminate it and create long-term prosperity.

The development of Haiti depends critically on the active participation of its diaspora. By means of investments, mentoring, and knowledge exchange, the Haitian diaspora can contribute to wealth generation. By investing in local businesses, providing financial support, and distributing their knowledge of technology, healthcare, and education, diaspora people can help Haiti grow.

Successful Haitian entrepreneurs abroad can inspire and help local talent through coaching programs, promoting an entrepreneurial culture in their homeland. The diaspora's financial resources, networks, and experience can enable Haiti to rebuild internal capacity for sustainable development and deepen its linkages to the world community. To eliminate poverty and create long-term wealth, Haiti must reimagine its future.

The country requires a comprehensive, multidimensional approach that supports health, education, governance, and economic inclusion. These foundational elements are vital for transforming the lives of millions of Haitians, moving from mere survival to a vision of shared prosperity. This metamorphosis consists in adopting a wealth-generating mindset. Though it may take time, Haiti's road to prosperity is doable with a clear vision and smart policies that will help eradicate poverty and generate inspiration and opportunity. Reaching a better future requires willpower and courage to overcome persistent challenges.

CHAPTER 14

HONORING SELF-DEPENDENCE, LABOR, PRODUCTIVITY, AND INNOVATION

Six days thou shall labor. Exodus 20:8

Personal and collective growth depends on innovation, productivity, labor, and self-reliance. These values lay a strong foundation for a rich, strong, and vibrant society. Haiti can overcome its challenges and unlock its people's potential upon such a foundation. Self-dependence is the cornerstone of empowerment; labor is the engine of progress; productivity is the key to growth; and innovation is the catalyst for thriving.

Self-dependence enables individuals and communities to rely on their resources, skills, and efforts to achieve their goals. This mindset is about developing a sense of self-reliance and interdependence and making decisions that directly impact the country. It is impossible to exaggerate the importance of self-reliance in the context of personal development. It fosters a sense of accountability and ownership, which motivates individuals to solve problems independently and pursue opportunities. Consequently, individuals cultivate a proactive approach to life and develop confidence.

Similarly, self-reliance enables a nation to establish its course, and execute policies that reflect its distinctive context and objectives. Self-reliance is the foundation of economic resilience and national sovereignty, allowing nations to flourish in adversity and withstand external shocks.

Empowered communities promote collaboration, resource sharing, and self-reliance. Transformational leadership prioritizes programs targeting long-term success to inspire community involvement. Cooperatives for crafts, agriculture, and services help communities pool resources, distribute risks, and gain from economies of scale.

Entrepreneurship is critical for a self-sustaining economy. Small enterprises can spur innovation, create jobs, and encourage economic development, making them essential for a functioning economy.

Labor is the driving force behind economic development and social advancement, ultimately leading to self-reliance. Cultural attitudes toward labor are firmly ingrained in Haiti's history and social fabric. Work is often viewed as a need and source of human dignity; however, attitudes toward different types of labor are frequently ambivalent. Manual labor has long been linked to poverty and lack of education, while occupations requiring advanced education or technical skills are highly valued.

The social stigma associated with manual labor derives from Haiti's history of slavery and severe working conditions for African slaves. This legacy helps to understand why some people find physical work unpleasant. Still, it's essential to change the narrative and value all forms of work.

Shifting social attitudes will support the dignity of all types of labor. This shift can benefit from national events and media, advocating for equitable pay and rights, and providing vocational training and skill development programs. Haiti can foster a culture that values all workers, regardless of occupation.

This valorization conforms to the International Labor Organization's respect for all labor. The ILO's Decent Work Agenda offers a framework for social debate, workplace rights, social protection, and employment generation. Such a framework will help labor unions, businesses, and the government work together to improve labor standards.

National holidays like Labor Day should honor workers' efforts in all spheres of the economy, and should not only be days off. Stories highlighting workers' achievements and efforts, public service announcements (PSAs) stressing the dignity of labor, and media campaigns featuring documentaries on several professions can all help foster a more positive view of work. The nation can boost living standards and encourage economic growth by raising labor force productivity. The sectors of the economy—which blend services, manufacturing, and agriculture—have different productivity levels. Such information will help spot areas for development and implement effective strategies.

Poor infrastructure, limited use of modern technologies, and small-scale farming all contribute to the agriculture industry's relatively low output. The small manufacturing sector has shown promise, especially in textiles and clothing. Still, it deals with outdated equipment, poor infrastructure, and a shortage of trained workers. Similarly, the services sector, encompassing tourism, commerce, and finance, struggles with an inadequate legislative framework, infrastructure, and limited access to technology.

Haiti must address these obstacles to improve productivity by implementing continuous professional development and training programs, increasing access to capital for small and medium enterprises, and making targeted investments in infrastructure and technology. Furthermore, a holistic approach is needed to address several challenges. Small and medium-sized businesses (SMEs) need access to funding via:

Microcredit: Small enterprises might get money to support projects for increasing production. Microloans help entrepreneurs buy tools, hire more staff, or grow their businesses.

Grants and Subsidies: Government grants and subsidies can help small and medium-sized enterprises (SMEs) develop training programs, infrastructure, and technology adoption.

Public–Private Partnerships: Fostering partnerships between

the public and private sectors can mobilize resources and expertise to assist SMEs. These partnerships facilitate access to funding, offer technical assistance, and generate opportunities for collaboration.

Customizing initiatives to certain regions and attending to focused needs can increase efficiency. These initiatives will raise living standards, boost economic growth in communities, and sharpen skills.

Innovation has brought notable social and economic progress in nations worldwide. The effective implementation of the Sustainable Development Goals depends on fostering a culture of creativity, technology, product and service development, which improves productivity and quality of life. Innovation has a transforming effect in many contexts, including grassroots innovations in rural India and Silicon Valley's technological successes.

Innovation leads to new product and service development, market growth, and higher competency. Its effects on environmental sustainability, education, and healthcare are amazing. R&D facilities, academic, industrial, and government cooperation, as well as finance and incubation for entrepreneurs, provide a supporting innovation ecosystem. Given today's fast-changing surroundings, flexibility is absolutely essential.

Starting innovative projects and companies depends on access to funding and incubation. Accelerators and incubators provide mentoring, funding, networking, and business growth assistance. Establishing a network of incubators and accelerators in Haiti will enable firms born out of creative ideas to flourish. Startups can thrive, generating employment and strengthening the economy. Co-working areas and innovation hubs let creators connect, access tools, and grow ideas.

These platforms encourage a creative environment by connecting people with similar interests. They stimulate small teams to provide answers for local problems. National innovation contests can produce innovative ideas, targeting agriculture, healthcare, and education sectors. Grants can offer the necessary funds to implement the winners' ideas.

Creativity and critical thinking in the classroom will help produce future inventors. An interactive and dynamic approach is needed to develop pupils' creative thinking and problem-solving ability. Extracurricular events such as scientific contests, robotics clubs, and innovation seminars can inspire student inventiveness and passion.

CHAPTER 15

RESTORING THE ENVIRONMENT AND ACHIEVING LAND REFORM

Look after the land, and the land will look after you; destroy the land, and it will destroy you. Aboriginal proverb

Environmental challenges pose a significant risk to Haiti's sustainable development. Once thriving with lush forests and fertile soils, the country now bears the scars of decades of environmental neglect and mismanagement, including deforested towering mountains and huge coastal plains. Pollution, deforestation, and soil deterioration have negatively impacted the environment and the well-being of the Haitian people.

There is a profound correlation between Haiti's socio-economic circumstances and its environmental degradation. Forest loss has resulted in severe soil erosion, which has reduced the amount of arable land available for agriculture and has contributed to food insecurity. The economic consequences of environmental decline have perpetuated cycles of poverty and inequality, while polluted rivers and streams have compromised the health of local communities. Ecological restoration and land reform are crucial for the nation's growth and prosperity.

Land reform contributes to solving environmental issues. In Haiti, land tenure has historically been inefficient and unequal, hindering sustainable development. Land monopolies and ambiguous tenure have led to widespread abuse and disputes.

Effective land reform is about social justice. It involves community, government, and international cooperation.

Haiti's ecosystem restoration and land reform require continuous commitment from every segment of society. A greener and fairer country sustains stability and progress.

Environmental degradation in Haiti began in the colonial era when forests were cut down to grow crops. Mass deforestation, which occurred to produce sugar, coffee, and other cash crops, persists today. It worsened following Haiti's independence to meet the demand for agricultural land, fuel wood for a growing population, and lumber sales to repay the unfairly imposed debt to France.

Less than 2 percent of Haiti's original forest cover is estimated to remain, a stark reminder of the long-term repercussions of unsustainable land use.

Alternative energy sources and sustainable agricultural practices can mitigate deforestation and its far-reaching and severe consequences. Losing tree cover causes soil erosion, which lowers the land's fertility and raises the risk of landslides. It also threatens human lives, infrastructure, and agricultural productivity. Without the canopy, the soil is depleted by the wind and rain. Heavy rain removes topsoil, which is necessary for agricultural development and fertility. Erosion lowers the land's yield and produces arid landscapes. Arable land loss worsens food insecurity and makes it difficult for farmers to reap adequate food for their families and communities.

Furthermore, environmental degradation affects water supplies. Deforestation and soil erosion cause rivers and streams to silt, reducing their size and capacity and raising flooding risk. Poor waste management practices contaminate water bodies and groundwater. Contaminated water sources bring high health risks to communities, including spreading diseases and decreasing availability of clean water for drinking and agricultural use.

The socioeconomic repercussions of Haiti's environmental

neglect are far-reaching. Degradation of natural resources directly influences the livelihoods of many people who rely heavily on agriculture. As agricultural output and soil fertility deteriorate, poverty and food insecurity worsen. Poor sanitation and dirty water sources can spread diseases and harm community health.

Environmental deterioration significantly impacts Haiti's agriculture sector, which is crucial to the economy. Farmers face significant challenges due to soil degradation, natural catastrophes, and climate change. Reduced agricultural production impacts food supply and economic stability in rural areas. As earnings decline and crops fail, individuals often shift to urban regions for a better life. This migration puts additional pressure on the already inadequate infrastructure and services available in the metropolitan areas. Sustainable land management and environmental restoration investments help upend these cycles and increase resilience and economic growth.

Land management programs must give top attention to land ownership. Peruvian economist Hernando de Soto argues that conferring property rights to the poor would benefit everyone, dramatically lifting a nation's economic activity[77]He studied land-related issues in Peru, Egypt, Haiti, and the Philippines. He noticed that disadvantaged individuals may take up to 19 years to obtain title to their land and homes. The process is complicated, costly, and time-consuming. Many poor people own houses without official titles. For low-income families, high real estate taxes often cause payment defaults.

Since gaining independence, Haiti has struggled with the consequences of the massive land grab. The exclusion of most of the population from the main economic circuit has fueled frustration and anger, affecting political stability, security, and the environment. Keeping this issue on the back burner is a recipe for continuous man-made disasters.

The property rights issue is only the tip of the iceberg.

[77] Soto, The Mystery of Capital.

Succession laws cause land fragmentation and entrench subsistence agriculture. The elites have imposed an exorbitant price on the country to keep their privileges. Their business model has resulted in economic stagnation and downfall. De Soto believes that elites may be educated and finally understand the benefits of land reforms. Given inevitable opposition, effective implementation of land reform in Haiti depends on wisdom and experience. Success calls for tenacity, openness, creative ideas, and abundant consultations.

A small elite under French colonial control kept large areas for plantation development, leaving most of the population with limited access to the means of production. Once independent in 1804, the recently established Haitian state faced land redistribution challenges. Former slaves made a patchwork of tiny, dispersed land claims for themselves.

Often possessing the most sought-after lands, the wealthy maintained the legacy of unequal land distribution from colonialism. Subsequent measures often encouraged the concentration of landownership, resulting in a legacy of unfairness that continues today.

Haiti attempted to modernize its land laws, but their implementation was inconsistent and ineffective. Efforts to redistribute land were hampered by opposition from powerful landowners and political instability. Governments' inability to create a consistent strategy for fair distribution caused land policy to become scattered over time, leading to the coexistence of large estates and small subsistence farms. Currently, land ownership is quite unequal, with a few wealthy individuals and institutions controlling most areas.

Many rural communities struggle with ownership insecurity and restricted investment in sustainable practices due to unclear legal titles for their small plots of land. Uncertainty in land tenure hinders development by discouraging long-term improvements and limiting financial access. The lack of good governance and complete land records contributes to land disputes and conflicts.

Many landowners feel vulnerable due to the lack of official documentation. Inefficient administrative systems and inadequate legal frameworks make it challenging to obtain clear titles. Farmers fear losing their property, hindering investment in sustainable agricultural practices, and land upgrades. Resolving land claims through the courts can be long and expensive.

Land injustice has far-reaching consequences. Small farmers find it difficult to make ends meet from their little acreage. Many look for greater opportunities in cities driven by poverty and food insecurity. Unplanned urbanization and migration aggravate social and financial inequalities, emphasizing the need for thorough land reform.

Fair access to land serves social justice, allowing every citizen to benefit from their nation's natural resources. Effective land reform gives farmers security and incentives to invest in their land, raising agricultural productivity. It can also help to combat climate change, lower environmental damage, and enhance sustainable land use. Land reform can increase social cohesion by removing land-related disputes and advancing justice and inclusion.

Land reform could boost farmers' access to credit by enabling them to invest in technology and inputs using their land as collateral. Farmers are more likely to improve their land, adopt sustainable methods, and increase yields when they have clear ownership or long-term leases. This will upgrade rural populations' livelihoods, food security, and earnings.

Land reform must accompany environmental restoration and sustainability. Including ecological elements into land reform will empower Haiti to build a strong and sustainable farming sector.

Afforestation and reforestation are important methods for rebuilding Haiti's ecology. Afforestation involves planting trees in new areas, while reforestation involves recovering trees in depleted areas. Both are important to restoring the nation's forest cover, enhancing soil stability, and raising biodiversity.

Successful reforestation and afforestation programs depend on community involvement. Local communities have a vested interest in the success of these initiatives and significant knowledge about their surroundings. Involving communities in tree-planting efforts fosters ownership and responsibility, ensuring long-term sustainability in reforested areas. Projects may provide seedlings, teach people how to plant and care for trees, and provide resources and technical support.

Effective reforestation and afforestation programs require strong government policies and international backing. The Haitian government can implement regulations that promote tree planting, protect existing forests, and penalize illegal logging. International cooperation can offer finance, technical expertise, and access to global best practices. Collaborating with NGOs, international organizations, and foreign governments can increase the scope and impact of reforestation activities.

Protecting and restoring watersheds and adopting sustainable irrigation practices are key components of this strategy. Watersheds help maintain water quality and availability. They require forests and vegetation cover as natural filters and buffers to reduce sedimentation and pollution in water bodies. Hence, reforestation, erosion control, and protected zones are imperative. Programs for community-based watershed management enable citizens to actively protect their local water supplies.

Sustainable irrigation systems help mitigate the effects of agriculture on water supplies by increasing water efficiency. Drip irrigation can help cut water wastage and feed water straight to plant roots. Rainwater harvesting systems supply water for agricultural use by gathering and storing. Training farmers and modernizing infrastructure can improve water management in farming.

Land reform promotes social equity, increases agricultural output, and ensures sustainable land use. It supports strong environmental policies. Effective land reform requires a comprehensive approach that includes legislative frameworks, participatory methods, and stakeholder collaboration.

Effective land reform requires a holistic strategy, including legal frameworks, participatory techniques, and stakeholder cooperation. Strong legal systems and policies guarantee unambiguous rights, safe tenure, and a fair share under an equitable and well-executed land reform using transparent and participatory methods. Inclusion requires thorough land surveys, community engagement into decision-making, and user-friendly land registration and dispute resolution procedures.

Drawing on effective land-reform initiatives elsewhere can give Haiti valuable insight. As South Korea and Taiwan show, thorough land reforms have helped rural growth and agricultural productivity.

These programs stressed supporting small producers, fostering community involvement, and ensuring legal clarity. Applying best practices in Haiti requires understanding the unique social, economic, and cultural aspects.

The government must set and enforce rules, offer technical support, and take a leadership role to effectively operate land-reform programs.

NGOs can provide expertise in sustainable land-management practices, facilitate community engagement, and advocate for land rights to play a supportive role. The legitimacy and success of land reform depend on the active involvement of local communities in the implementation process.

Opposition from those who profit from the current status quo may obstruct the land reform process. Overcoming this challenge calls for political resolve and public backing. Stakeholder communication, public education, and advocacy campaigns help increase land reform's support and understanding of its advantages.

Land reform aims to empower communities by educating them on their land rights, equipping them with the necessary tools and resources to improve agriculture, and guaranteeing their voices are heard. Participatory mapping and community land trusts are two instances of community-based land management projects that enable people to take ownership of their resources.

Long-term objectives and benchmarks will help evaluate land reform. Consistent monitoring and evaluation are crucial for making required changes and determining their impact.

Logistical and financial challenges will stand in the way. Land reform and environmental restoration require sizeable investments in technology, human capital, and new infrastructure. Logistical issues include land registration and survey completion, as well as using the proper technology and system.

Furthermore, social and cultural obstacles can impede environmental rehabilitation and land reform efforts. Changing deeply ingrained social conventions and traditional landownership systems can prove difficult. To overcome these challenges, communities must be included in the planning and execution stages.

Achieving environmental restoration and land reform in Haiti is a challenging but feasible objective requiring strategic actions, committed stakeholders, and a clear vision. Haiti's future is promising, and its vision is a restored environment characterized by fertile soils, flourishing forests, and clean, abundant water resources. This vision includes a reformed land-ownership system characterized by sustainable land-use practices, secure tenure, and equitably distributed land.

Additionally, economic development, resilience to climate change, social justice, and environmental sustainability will enable all citizens to reap the benefits of the nation's natural resources and contribute to its progress.

Effective land reform guarantees fair access, advances social justice, and gives underprivileged people power. Safe land tenure fosters sustainable agricultural practices, higher productivity, and rural growth. Haiti can rebuild its natural ecosystem and create economic and social resilience through land reform and environmental restoration initiatives, including reforestation, afforestation, soil conservation, and sustainable water management.

Land reform and environmental restoration will empower Haiti to develop into a country of opportunity, hope, and resilience for future generations. The country's growth and welfare depend on a relentless dedication to these underrated imperatives.

CHAPTER 16
DEVELOPING TOURISM AS A MAIN SECTOR

Tourism is a powerful vehicle for economic growth and job creation all over the world. David Scowsill, former President and CEO of the World Travel & Tourism Council

Tourism is among the most potent engines driving economic development in the modern world. It affects almost every aspect of life and provides direct and indirect benefits, including generating millions of jobs and stimulating local businesses. Tourism has transformative power for countries like Haiti, with excellent unrealized potential in natural beauty, vibrant culture, and historical significance. It sustains economic diversification, cultural regeneration, and improved international status. The government must prioritize tourism in line with its national development agenda.

Haiti's rich history has impacted the Caribbean and the world. The nation features impressive mountains, pristine beaches, and a dynamic culture. Its topography, cultural legacy, and resilience make it a perfect candidate for tourism growth. Still, internal conflicts and external perception cause this potential to remain unrealized. Developing tourism as a major industry would help Haiti start a transforming path, honing its cultural identity, and using natural resources to release economic development.

Haiti is in the Caribbean, one of the world's most popular tourism destinations. This region is known for its biodiversity, gorgeous coastlines, and blue oceans. Its closeness to North America and Europe, two main markets for international travelers, provides a significant strategic advantage. This location can contribute to efforts to restore its status as a vacation destination offering sun, adventure, and cultural experiences.

Haiti has a comparative advantage with its diverse landscape and unique historical significance. Its famous sites, such as Sans-Souci Palace and the Citadelle Laferrière, evoke the nation's fight for freedom and its first Black republic status. In addition to rich music, dance, and art, these monuments provide a cultural experience unlike any other.

The country's proximity to the United States makes visiting convenient for tourists. Haiti's restoration to peace and stability, improved infrastructure, and transit choices will make it a popular holiday destination for Americans, Canadians, and Europeans seeking a typical Caribbean experience.

Haiti's tourist sector is still in its early stages, unlike Jamaica and the Dominican Republic, which have established robust tourism industries through government initiatives and private investment. However, this infancy provides an opportunity for creativity and development.

Haiti can stand out in the Caribbean tourism market by emphasizing its cultural and historical significance and natural beauty. Its geographical advantage is invaluable, but it must take intentional steps to become a vital player in the region's tourist economy.

Developing tourism as a key economic sector in Haiti offers long-term benefits beyond immediate cash rewards. Tourism has the potential to revolutionize Haiti's economy by generating sustainable income, jobs, and investment in key infrastructure. This industry promotes cultural preservation and environmental sustainability, laying the groundwork for sustainable prosperity and honoring the country's rich legacy. Focusing on tourism will diversify the economy, increase revenue, and transform local communities.

Haiti's economy relies heavily on agriculture and informal trade, which are sensitive sectors to exogenous shocks like natural disasters and market changes. Tourism will lessen reliance on traditional industries as a revenue source.

Tourist arrivals will boost activities in hospitality, shopping, transportation, and other industries. The economy will gain strength because of fresh resources and opportunities.

Tourism creates jobs that fit different degrees of skill. From entry-level jobs in hotels, restaurants, and tour operations to management and administrative roles in tourist companies, the tourism industry presents a career path that benefits urban and rural communities.

This engine tackles unemployment, especially among the youth population. From small guesthouses to tour guide services, tourism will allow locals to start businesses. A business-friendly policy can stimulate growth in other tourism-related sectors, such as agriculture and handicrafts.

One of the most immediate implications of tourism expansion is improved infrastructure. Attracting many visitors will require improved public services, utilities, and transportation investments. These improvements will enhance the tourists' experience and help the local communities. Visitors expect access to modern roadways, airports and terminals, consistent electricity and water supply, and healthcare facilities. Tourism-driven infrastructure development can improve the quality of life for every Haitian, particularly in rural areas where infrastructure usually lags behind metropolitan agglomerations. Investing in digital technologies and innovation will help improve the economy's general global competitiveness and efficiency.

Tourism can preserve and advance Haiti's rich legacy. While mass tourist models prioritize leisure and luxury, cultural tourism emphasizes history, traditions, and creativity. In addition to the beaches, the country offers visitors quality art, music, and events.

Tourism can help preserve historical sites. Cultural events, guided tours, and admission fees, which support local artists, singers, and craftspeople, will help conserve gems like the Citadelle Laferrière and the 365 Door Palace, keeping them in good condition for future generations.

As climate change threatens everyone, environmental preservation takes center stage worldwide. Haiti may present itself as a leader in sustainable tourism. The nation's reforested mountains, beaches, unique ecosystems, and other natural beauty can draw tourists and promote long-term sustainability policy.

Environmental care and sustainable tourism plans, including hotels and resorts with renewable energy sources, will help protect Haiti's natural resources. These initiatives maintain the ecology and draw environmentally sensitive visitors. The country can guarantee a fair sharing of tourism advantages by including local communities in eco-tourism initiatives. Profits will even increase with environmental preservation and community development.

Haiti must embrace smart policies and supportive attitudes to realize its tourism potential. Tourism development calls for a coordinated strategy that includes government support, business sector investment, community involvement, and safety and security policies.

Enhancing the nation's image overseas through robust marketing initiatives might help overcome prior perceptions and show Haiti as a dynamic and appealing destination. A well-defined national tourist strategy guides development and investment efforts. The strategy should aim for long-term sustainability, including cultural preservation, environment-friendly activities, and short-term benefits, including enhancement of tourism attractions.

Tourism growth also depends heavily on a business-friendly legislative framework. The government must develop the private sector and manage travel growth sensibly. While zoning limits help preserve natural resources from overdevelopment, tax benefits might lure foreign investors to create resorts. Strong government commitment to infrastructure development, legislative change, and worldwide promotion can propel notable increases in the tourism industry.

Safety is paramount to any tourist destination. Travelers want secure and fun places to relax and explore. Haiti should prioritize safety for local people and foreign guests. It should also improve law enforcement to reduce crime rates. As observed at popular locations, the government can deploy well-trained tourist police patrols to maintain tourist security.

Safety includes transportation networks, water cleanliness, and international health standards for restaurants and hotels. Visitors want reliable emergency assistance and excellent healthcare facilities and response systems.

In terms of safety, perception is as vital as reality. Haiti's standing in the world media has sometimes resulted in a poor image overseas. Changing this perception requires better safety on the ground and aggressive marketing of these changes. Once visitors see Haiti as a safe and friendly place, they will come in increasing numbers.

An extensive and well-coordinated marketing campaign will be essential to establish Haiti as a major tourism destination. Travel blogs, social media, influencer relationships, trade shows—traditional and modern media—are all part of tourism marketing. These outlets will highlight Haiti's unique attractions, which include its history, culture, natural beauty, and hospitable people.

Establishing credibility and worldwide recognition requires an active participation in organizations such as the World Tourism Organization (UNWTO) and the Caribbean Tourism Organization (CTO). To provide packages and incentives, Haiti has to partner with travel operators, airlines, and cruise lines. This strategy will make visiting Haiti rather than another place more appealing and practical.

Developing a solid internet presence is vital in marketing.

Inaccurate and difficult-to-get information can discourage potential visitors from visiting a place. Essential is a well-designed national tourist website featuring interesting content, easy registration procedures, and helpful travel advice.

Inaccurate and difficult-to-access information can deter prospective tourists from visiting a destination. A well-designed national tourist website with helpful travel information, simple registration processes, and compelling content is essential. Creating a consistent and positive story can help Haiti shed its negative image and establish itself as a desirable destination.

Tourism development is a shared responsibility, and public-private partnerships (PPPs) are essential to creating a robust tourism sector. Although the government is instrumental in providing regulatory framework and infrastructure, private sector investment is vital in developing hotels, resorts, restaurants, and other tourism-related businesses. The tourism sector's long-term growth and increasing benefits depend on collaboration among local communities, businesses, and governmental agencies.

The government can facilitate low-interest loans, subsidies, and tax breaks to inspire private sector involvement in tourism initiatives. By removing red tape associated with business registration, permits, and foreign investment, Haiti will become more appealing to investors. The active involvement of both domestic and international investors who recognize the potential for long-term returns in the tourism sector has been key to the success of numerous Caribbean tourism destinations.

The private sector can also support community-based tourism projects that benefit local residents. Hotels and tour companies can team up with nearby artists, guides, and cultural organizations to offer travel experiences honoring Haiti's legacy. This approach guarantees sustainable and mutually beneficial tourism by supporting inclusive economic development and community ownership.

Past tourism experiences in Haiti bring attention to the

advantages and disadvantages of depending on this industry for national development. Known as the "Pearl of the Antilles," Haiti attracted international stars, artists, and culture-minded visitors during the 1950s and 1960s. But the political unrest that ended the golden age caused a sharp drop in tourist numbers. Political unrest and natural disasters like the 2010 earthquake have hampered attempts to reestablish the tourism industry.

The development of sustainable tourism calls for a stable political climate, open government, investment in infrastructure and attractions, and continuous efforts to improve security and safety. Authorities and stakeholders should avoid repeating mistakes to create a strong tourism industry that can withstand external shocks.

Innovation offers memorable, immersive, and significant experiences in today's competitive global travel market. Haiti provides unique experiences anchored in its rich history and culture. Among other digital technologies, interactive maps, mobile platforms, and virtual tours can improve visitor experiences and draw tech-savvy tourists.

Haiti can bank on tourism based on culture, adventure, and ecology. Eco-tourism has seen notable expansion worldwide as travelers choose sites offering sustainable activities and unspoiled natural surroundings. Haiti's mountainous landscapes and coastal areas are ideal for developing eco-friendly tourism.

In the same vein, adventure tourism, which encompasses cultural excursions, diving, and hiking, has the potential to appeal to younger travelers who are seeking unique experiences.

Local knowledge in tourism management is crucial to reintegrating Haiti into the global tourism market. To build a robust tourism sector, well-trained staff must supply high-quality services that match or exceed international standards. A successful tourism industry requires hospitality, customer service, marketing, destination management, and cultural preservation expertise.

Haiti can learn from other nations that have successfully

improved their economies by prioritizing tourism to overcome development challenges. Success stories flow from strategic planning, political will, a great dedication to preserving cultural assets, and infrastructure improvement. There are long-term advantages to increasing visitor numbers in Haiti. Tourism can transform the economy through job creation, encouragement of entrepreneurship, infrastructure improvement, and foreign investment attraction.

Haiti can boost its tourism industry by promoting eco-friendly offers, integrating locals in initiatives, and supporting small enterprises. Tourism can help boost the economy and highlight the country's beauty, resilience, and unique culture. With the correct vision and action, Haiti can become a cultural tourism hub, offering visitors an unforgettable experience.

CHAPTER 17

LEVERAGING ARTIFICIAL INTELLIGENCE FOR THE DEVELOPMENT OF HAITI

AI is going to change the world more than anything in the history of humanity. More than electricity. Kai-Fu Lee, businessman, computer scientist, investor, and writer.

Artificial Intelligence (AI) is leading a transformational surge in global technological developments. AI can change nation-building, governance, and development strategies by mimicking human intelligence, evaluating big data, and rendering autonomous conclusions. AI may increase state capability in countries like Haiti, boost democratic rule, and streamline nation-building.

Nation-building in the twenty-first century transcends conventional infrastructure and institutional framework. A digital ecosystem can help produce fresh ideas for challenging problems. Artificial intelligence can contribute to building better infrastructure, urban design, and public services. Haiti can hope to build smart cities, adequate public transportation, and efficient use of available resources to facilitate long-term growth.

AI can significantly enhance democratic governance based on social equity and political stability. Democracy rests on fair and transparent electoral processes, citizen engagement, and accountable governance. Haiti's democratic experience will benefit from AI technologies, including blockchain for secure voting, machine learning for electoral fraud detection, and natural language processing for public sentiment analysis.

It is impossible to overstate AI's significance in advancing development. A stable and resilient state necessitates effective law enforcement, robust security measures, and efficient government operations. AI-driven automation, predictive analytics, and advanced surveillance systems can expedite administrative processes, enhance public safety, and combat crime, reinforcing state institutions' capabilities.

Another area in which AI has significant potential is economic development, a critical component of nation-building. AI has the potential to significantly enhance Haiti's economy by revolutionizing agriculture and healthcare, transforming education, and nurturing entrepreneurship. By implementing AI technologies, Haiti can foster innovation, create job opportunities, and increase productivity, thereby establishing a diverse and dynamic economy.

However, incorporating artificial intelligence in Haiti's development plan presents certain challenges. A robust legislative framework addressing data privacy and algorithmic bias is necessary to guarantee the ethical use of artificial intelligence technologies. Effective artificial intelligence deployment calls for infrastructure building, public-private cooperation establishment, and knowledge and talent development.

AI will significantly impact Haiti's economic development, state strength, democratic governance, and nation-building. Global examples show AI's ability to create a sustainable and affluent future. Understanding the benefits and challenges of AI can help Haitian stakeholders adopt this disruptive technology and drive tremendous development for the nation.

Nation-building is establishing a national identity through infrastructure, institutions, and a common culture. Today's technology enhances living standards, accelerates procedures, and advances environmentally friendly development. Nation-building calls for physical infrastructure, social cohesion, economic growth, and a common future vision.

Artificial intelligence can speed up progress in urban planning. Predictive analytics and machine learning techniques are AI tools that increase efficiency and sustainability. Through artificial intelligence, smart city projects can maximize waste management systems, lower energy consumption, and control traffic flows, thus creating more livable and sustainable urban environments. Predictive maintenance—another artificial intelligence application—can monitor the state of infrastructure, including roadways and bridges, to predict the required maintenance to avoid expensive accidents and repairs.

Artificial intelligence (AI) can enhance catastrophe readiness and response by means of natural disaster forecast, route optimization for evacuation, and resource management, to protect property and lives.

The potential transformative effects of AI on public services and utilities in Haiti are significant. AI can assist public agencies in providing citizens with more efficient services by automating routine tasks and providing data-driven insights. In the healthcare sector, AI-powered diagnostic tools and telemedicine platforms have the potential to enhance healthcare delivery, particularly in remote areas, and manage health records while predicting disease outbreaks.

AI can provide real-time feedback, personalize learning environments, and assist educators in spotting and helping challenged students. Predictive policing, sophisticated surveillance systems, and better emergency response coordination all help public safety. Real-time weather forecasts, pest detection, and crop management have helped Kenya's AI-powered agricultural systems increase productivity and resilience. This experience emphasizes the importance of scalability and local adaptation.

Haiti can also adapt artificial intelligence technologies to its particular context and needs. Public-private cooperation has enabled other nations to carry out artificial intelligence initiatives. Significant training and education investments must develop local artificial intelligence capabilities. Haiti needs a strategic vision that includes infrastructure development, law and regulation, capacity building, and public-private partnerships to use AI for nation-building. Funding digital infrastructure, including data centers and fast internet, will help artificial intelligence applications grow more rapidly.

A national AI strategy should have well-defined objectives, priorities, and execution plans, supported by a strong legal framework to guarantee the ethical use of AI, data protection, and security. AI can significantly advance democracy, political stability and social justice. AI technology can improve Haiti's democracy by fostering inclusive participation, eliminating fraud, and increasing transparency, leading to better accountability.

AI can promote citizen participation by providing venues for direct contact between the government and citizens. AI-powered chatbots and virtual assistants can offer real-time information and services, making government more accessible. These platforms enable the collection of public comments and suggestions, guiding legislators and other leaders in making better decisions. Natural language processing systems track public opinion on different subjects through social media and communication channels. This helps the government meet people's needs.

Haiti can benefit from valuable insights provided by successful implementations of AI in democratic governance around the globe. The Estonian e-Residency program leverages artificial intelligence (AI) to provide secure digital identities to its citizens, thereby enabling online voting and other government services. The initiative has enhanced the transparency of the country's democratic process.

Brazil AI-powered technologies provide real-time insights into popular sentiment and potential difficulties monitoring and analyzing social media during elections. These instances highlight the revolutionary power of AI in democratic governance.

Another critical component of incorporating AI into democratic governance is capacity building. Education and training programs are essential for creating a productive workforce capable of managing and implementing AI technology. These programs train government officials, election professionals, and other stakeholders to use AI technologies and systems.

Public-private partnerships can greatly advance democratic governance driven by artificial intelligence. Cooperation among academia, business, and government will help to share knowledge, resources, and experience. While technological companies provide artificial intelligence solutions, academic institutions can assist research and training initiatives. Promoting private sector investment in AI technologies for governance can further stimulate innovation and development.

Haiti can enhance stability, security, and efficient governance. AI will boost the capacity of state institutions by streamlining law enforcement, bolstering security, and improving government efficiency. Implementing AI technologies can improve governmental functions, benefit residents, and drive national growth.

AI can enhance law enforcement and public security. Predictive policing, an AI tool, helps law enforcement agencies better allocate resources and prevent crime by studying historical data to forecast future crimes. AI-powered surveillance systems can enhance situational awareness and response capabilities by monitoring public locations, detecting suspicious activity, and alerting authorities in real time. AI can improve national security by evaluating intelligence data, recognizing dangers, and facilitating strategic planning.

Haiti can learn from countries that have successfully implemented AI. Singapore's government has used AI to improve public services and streamline processes. The Smart Nation initiative uses AI to improve public safety, monitor air quality, and control traffic, resulting in a more efficient and livable city.

Predictive policing initiatives driven by artificial intelligence in cities like Los Angeles and Chicago have produced reduced crime rates and better law enforcement efficacy. These examples show how profoundly artificial intelligence is changing government operations. Industries including agriculture, healthcare, education, and business could be revolutionized by artificial intelligence (AI), therefore fostering higher production, employment, and innovation.

Though it raises ethical data privacy and security concerns, artificial intelligence can change Haiti's economy and society. AI systems use large volumes of data, including sensitive personal information. Protecting privacy rights depends on guaranteeing safe personal data collection, storage, and processing. In Haiti, where digital infrastructure is still developing, robust cybersecurity standards and data protection rules are crucial. To avoid data breaches and illegal access, procedures should align with international standards and include public awareness initiatives that educate citizens on their rights and data privacy.

Bias and impartiality in AI are additional serious considerations. AI systems can perpetuate and amplify prejudices when trained with biased data, exacerbate existing disparities, and unfairly treat certain groups. AI systems must be fairly designed and implemented. Monitoring results continuously is important to improve AI performance, as is using varied data sets for training and testing algorithms for bias. To ensure that AI technologies promote equity and inclusion, policies addressing and mitigating prejudice must be implemented.

Regulatory frameworks must be agile and forward-thinking to keep up with the rapidly evolving AI technology. The Haitian government should collaborate with international organizations and local stakeholders to create comprehensive AI legislation that promotes ethical use, accountability, and transparency. Defined protocols can help mitigate the negative effects of AI applications by establishing clear accountability procedures. AI's potential social repercussions require ethical consideration, including regulating economic imbalances, social institutions, and employment.

While AI has the potential to create new work opportunities, it may also lead to the displacement of certain occupations, especially those with repetitive tasks.

Establishing workforce transition measures, such as retraining and upskilling programs, is crucial to ensure people don't fall behind in the AI-driven economy. To avoid exacerbating existing social and economic inequities, inclusive policies should be devised to ensure equitable distribution of AI benefits across society.

Haiti needs a holistic approach to using artificial intelligence for nation-building, democratic governance, state strengthening, and economic development. The road map addresses infrastructure, policy making, capacity growth, and public-private cooperation.

Assessing development, spotting obstacles, and adjusting the strategy of the AI program's impact depends on constant monitoring and evaluation. Establishing an autonomous body to supervise AI initiatives and enforce ethical standards will help improve accountability and openness. This body should routinely document the results of artificial intelligence initiatives, together with comments and suggestions for continuous development.

Knowledge sharing and international cooperation will support Haiti's artificial intelligence capacity to be in line with world trends. Collaboration with global technology businesses, research institutions, and international forums can provide essential resources and insights. By establishing itself as an active member of the global AI community, Haiti will attract investment, promote innovation, and remain informed about technological advancements.

Incorporating Artificial Intelligence (AI) into Haiti's

development strategy offers an unparalleled opportunity to transform the nation in multiple dimensions. Implementing a comprehensive and strategic AI integration strategy can produce significant benefits. AI can help Haiti achieve a sustainable and successful future by enhancing democracy, strengthening governmental institutions, and driving economic development.

CHAPTER 18

THE PLACE OF HAITI IN THE WORLD

Your long-term happiness and fulfillment depend on your ability to fulfill your soul's unique purpose and to fill the place in the world that only you can fill, making the contribution that only you can make.[78] *Rod Stryker, writer and meditation teacher*

Haiti has marked the annals of world history, as it brought to pass the first successful slave revolt, thus becoming the first sovereign Black republic in 1804. This significant event signaled the end of colonial rule in Haiti and served as a source of inspiration and hope for oppressed nations and enslaved individuals worldwide. Haiti's considerable role in the global narrative of human rights and liberation derives from its fight for freedom and eventual victory against one of the most powerful colonial empires at that time, namely France.

In addition to human rights and freedom, Haiti's international values encompass resilience, non-intervention, peaceful conflict resolution, cultural preservation, and non-indifference in the face of disasters. Throughout history, these ideals have shaped the country's diplomatic attitude, actions, and alliances. Haiti has consistently supported nations fighting against colonialism and oppression.

In the 19th century, Haiti supported Latin American

[78] Stryker, The Four Desires.

independence movements, particularly those led by Simón Bolívar. Haiti's foreign policy prioritizes non-intervention and respect for national sovereignty, which is informed by past experiences with occupation and interference. The government routinely promotes this principle at regional and international institutions, including the Organization of American States (OAS) and the United Nations (UN). In 1986, Haiti and other Caribbean and Latin American nations advocated for diplomatic engagement, mediation, and peaceful resolution of Nicaragua's internal conflict, rather than military action.

Haiti adheres to the United Nations Charter's principles of peaceful dispute resolution and respect for other states' sovereignty. This approach stems from recognizing that stability and harmony are indispensable for advancing regional and international affairs. Therefore, the nation consistently advocates for dialogue and mediation, encouraging nations to refrain from military intervention and prioritize diplomatic solutions that preserve global peace and security.

Haiti is a founding member of the United Nations (UN), the Organization of American States (OAS), the Association of Caribbean States, and the Organisation Internationale de la Francophonie (OIF). This commitment to multilateral diplomacy flows from the principle that dialogue and diplomacy should take precedence over using force.

Haiti's foreign policy prioritizes non-indifference, demonstrating a commitment to humanitarian ideals and solidarity in man-made crises like war and genocide. With its history of overcoming oppression and humanitarian crises, Haiti strongly supports international efforts to end suffering from conflicts and atrocities. This policy guides Haiti's participation in international forums and its support for collective action to combat crimes against humanity.

As a country with a history of migration and a sizeable diaspora, Haiti actively advocates for the protection of refugees and internally displaced people in situations of conflict. It endorses the Responsibility to Protect (R2P) doctrine, which asserts that the international community is obligated to prevent genocide, war crimes, ethnic cleansing, and crimes against humanity. Haiti's endorsement of R2P indicates its commitment to non-indifference in situations where governments fail to safeguard their populations, although R2P is occasionally a source of disagreement among nations that are wary of foreign intervention. For Haiti, sovereignty does not override the need to prevent atrocities and protect human lives.

Resilience has become a fundamental part of Haiti's identity, especially given its vulnerability to natural disasters. Haiti's commitment to resilience extends to its foreign policy, where it actively collaborates with other countries and international bodies on disaster preparedness and response. Through partnerships and forums, including the Caribbean Disaster Emergency Management Agency (CDEMA), Haiti shares best practices and advocates for more comprehensive regional disaster strategies. Haiti's leadership in promoting resilience demonstrates its dedication to safeguarding communities and supporting other vulnerable nations.

Haiti values cultural preservation as a diplomatic principle, recognizing that culture fosters national cohesion and strengthens international bonds. This focus is especially evident in Haiti's close relationship with Francophone countries and its active participation in the International Organization of La Francophonie (OIF). Haiti works with other French-speaking nations to promote cultural exchange, language preservation, and educational support through the OIF. During the annual Francophonie Summit, Haiti advocates for development programs that help protect linguistic diversity and cultural heritage, reflecting its commitment to preserving cultural identity as an essential aspect of global cooperation.

Social justice and economic equity are key aspects of Haiti's international values, stemming from its founding principles of equality and shared prosperity. Haiti consistently advocates for fair economic practices and has engaged in global dialogues to address wealth inequality. This commitment likely derives from the country's domestic struggles with social exclusion. In forums like the United Nations, Haiti supports policies that favor economic inclusion and provide opportunities for marginalized communities, seeking to bridge the gap between wealthier and poorer nations.

All these values that sustain Haiti's diplomatic action reflect its unique history and commitment to dignity, respect, and collective progress on the world stage. Understanding Haiti's place in the world requires a recognition of its profound historical contributions as a symbol of resistance and a pioneer in the fight for equality and justice.

Haiti's geopolitical significance is also a key aspect of its foreign policy. Strategically located in the Caribbean, Haiti has always been important in regional politics and international relations. Its proximity to major sea routes and neighboring countries like the Dominican Republic and Cuba has influenced its interactions and alliances. Haiti's membership in various international organizations, such as the United Nations, the Organization of American States (OAS), and the Caribbean Community (CARICOM), underscores its role in global diplomacy and regional cooperation. These relationships have allowed Haiti to engage in international dialogues, advocate for its interests, and contribute to collective efforts addressing regional and global challenges.

Haiti has exerted considerable influence in regional politics. One of Haiti's most important geopolitical relations is with its neighbor, the Dominican Republic, which shares the island of Hispaniola. There have been times of friction and cooperation throughout the two countries' lengthy and complex history. Their shared location compels cooperation on trade, immigration, and environmental management despite cultural and economic divides. The ups and downs of efforts to improve bilateral ties and resolve shared issues underscore how crucial their interdependence is.

These countries have difficulty living together, yet they cannot live separately from each other.

Haiti's proximity to Cuba also significantly influences its geopolitical landscape. The relationship between Haiti and Cuba has been characterized by mutual support, particularly in healthcare and education. Cuban medical teams have provided invaluable assistance to Haiti, especially in times of crisis, fostering a bond that transcends political ideologies. This relationship underscores Haiti's ability to forge alliances, contributing to its national development and resilience.

Haiti's Caribbean membership in the Community (CARICOM) is particularly significant for its regional integration and economic cooperation. Through CARICOM, the country participates in programs that promote commerce, economic expansion, and social advancement. Haiti benefits from its membership in promoting its interests, exchanging best practices, and gaining from initiatives to tackle regional issues like disaster relief and climate change.

Haiti prioritizes economic, technical, and South-South cooperation as a cornerstone of its foreign policy, viewing these forms of cooperation as a crucial stepping stone to resilience, self-sufficiency, and sustainable development. Given that it enables the exchange of resources, expertise, and innovations that tackle shared issues without depending on conventional donor-country models, South-South cooperation resonates with Haiti's commitment to solidarity among developing nations.

In economic cooperation, Haiti has engaged in partnerships emphasizing trade, access to financial resources, and the mutual benefits of regional market integration, especially with its Caribbean and Latin American neighbors. Through collaborations with countries like Cuba, Brazil, and Venezuela, Haiti has benefited from expertise and resources that improve its local capabilities and infrastructure. South-South cooperation, more broadly, offers Haiti a platform to work collaboratively with countries that understand and share its developmental challenges, creating opportunities for mutual advancement that respect each nation's sovereignty and unique needs.

Haiti's foreign policy prioritizes relations with key stakeholders such as the United States, Canada, the Dominican Republic, Venezuela, Cuba, Mexico, Brazil, Chile, France, Germany, Spain, Japan, and Taiwan to advance development, foster economic cooperation, enhance regional security, and uphold its sovereignty. Although in need of streamlining to redirect funding to pressing domestic issues, these partnerships offer Haiti opportunities that are vital for addressing its complex challenges, including poverty, political instability, and natural disasters. Here's how Haiti prioritizes and engages with each of these key stakeholders.

The United States is Haiti's largest trading partner and primary source of foreign aid, making it a critical ally in Haiti's foreign policy. Following the 2010 earthquake, the US government and private organizations provided billions in aid for humanitarian assistance, infrastructure reconstruction, and development. Haiti depends heavily on the US for imports, remittances, and investment, which drive its economy. The US provides security support, working with Haitian authorities to combat gang violence and improve stability. While this relationship is essential for Haiti's economic survival, it is not without tension, particularly regarding Haitian sovereignty and the extent of US influence over domestic policy.

Canada is another prominent ally, recognized for its consistent support of development aid, governance, and security. Canada's assistance spans sectors such as education, health, and women's empowerment. Its influence allows it to play a stabilizing role in Haitian policy and economic initiatives.

The Dominican Republic is Haiti's closest neighbor and one of its most significant economic partners. Despite a complex history, the two countries share deep economic ties, with significant cross-border trade, agriculture, commerce, and labor interdependence.

The relationship between Haiti and Venezuela holds profound historical and strategic significance, rooted in shared ideals of independence, solidarity, and mutual support. Haiti's assistance to Simón Bolívar during his quest for Latin American liberation in the nineteenth century established a foundation of solidarity between the two nations. This bond deepened in the twenty-first century with the PetroCaribe Agreement, which enabled Haiti to purchase oil from Venezuela at reduced prices, allowing the Haitian government to invest the savings in critical social and infrastructure programs.

Through PetroCaribe, Venezuela extended support that empowered Haiti to address pressing domestic needs, from healthcare to education. This highlights a model of South-South cooperation that prioritizes development and resilience. These relations underscore the importance of regional solidarity, demonstrating how alliances based on shared history and mutual respect can drive meaningful socio-economic progress and reinforce Haiti's connection with the wider Latin American community.

The relationship between Haiti and Cuba is a model of solidarity and South-South cooperation, characterized by cooperation in healthcare and education. Since the 1990s, Cuba has sent medical teams to Haiti, with Cuban doctors and healthcare professionals providing essential medical care, especially in rural and underserved areas. Cuba helps train Haitian doctors and medical students, to strengthen healthcare over the long term. This partnership has been invaluable during crises, such as the 2010 earthquake and cholera outbreak, where Cuban medical teams helped save lives and provide relief.

The educational exchange is equally significant, with literacy cooperation efforts and Cuban scholarships enabling Haitian students to pursue degrees in various fields. Through these sustained initiatives, the Haiti-Cuba relationship exemplifies a commitment to shared development, empowering Haiti while fostering regional unity based on mutual respect.

Brazil and Chile emerged as significant partners for Haiti through their active role in the United Nations Stabilization Mission in Haiti (MINUSTAH), which operated from 2004 to 2017 to stabilize Haiti after political crises. This partnership provides Haiti with allies in Latin America that understand its challenges, offering both diplomatic support and technical expertise that align with Haiti's foreign policy of regional solidarity and cooperative security. At the same time, many Haitian nationals have migrated to Brazil and Chile, expanding Haiti's diaspora and opportunities for remittances.

France holds a unique position in Haiti's foreign policy due to historical ties dating back to colonial times. While this relationship is complex, given Haiti's history as a former colony, it has evolved into a partnership characterized by cultural diplomacy. France remains committed to supporting Haiti's cultural heritage and Francophone identity, funding educational programs, and offering technical assistance. France's cultural influence in Haiti is significant, supporting language preservation and academic exchanges.

Other partners, including Spain, Germany, Japan, and Taiwan, prioritize humanitarian and development support for Haiti. These countries have offered scholarships and also supported development projects.

Haiti's relationship with Taiwan is significant, as Taiwan provides Haiti with financial aid, technical expertise, and agricultural support. Haiti is one of the few countries that diplomatically recognize Taiwan, and this recognition has fostered a strong bilateral partnership. Taiwan has funded many projects in

Haiti, from energy infrastructure, such as solar power projects, to healthcare advancements and agricultural training. In return, Haiti's acknowledgement of Taiwan enhances Taiwan's diplomatic standing internationally, fostering a win-win partnership.

Haiti's foreign policy toward these key partners demonstrates its strategic approach to striking a balance between ties that support economic stability, sovereignty, and sustainable development. Haiti aspires to promote relationships that give mutual benefit and long-term impact, demonstrating its commitment to growth, stability, and dignity in a world where cooperation often comes with conditionalities.

Haiti's place in the world is deeply rooted in its unique history, vibrant culture, and resilient spirit. Understanding Haiti's geopolitical significance, its economic contributions, and the challenges it faces provides a comprehensive view of its current position on the global stage. Haiti's active participation in regional and international organizations, its cultural impact through art, literature, and music, and its ongoing commitment to human rights and democracy highlight its influential role in the world.

Haiti's historical achievements embody an enduring idea: the relentless pursuit of freedom, dignity, and resilience against overwhelming odds. The triumph of the Haitian revolution signals courage and self-determination. Despite its challenges, Haiti reminds the world of the importance of freedom, the richness of cultural identity, and the beauty of resilience, making it far more than just a country on the global map.

CHAPTER 19

LOVE NEVER FAILS

Love does not delight in evil but rejoices with the truth. It always protects, always trusts, always hopes, always perseveres. Love never fails. 1 Cor 13:6-8

Haiti has reached such a low point in its history that only a collective, burning desire like the state of mind that led to independence will produce its rebirth. Every Haitian can play a role in this regard. Every Haitian must love their fellow Haitians, engage in transforming Haiti, and show gratitude for what still works well.

In his book The Hidden Messages in Water, Japanese author Masaru Emoto provides evidence for the power of love and gratitude. The liquid produced beautiful crystals when words of love and gratefulness were spoken to a water container. When words of hatred and violence were used, the crystals were deformed. The same experience worked for rice. In time, words of love and gratitude produced a nicely fermented aroma, while words of hatred and violence caused a rotten smell. If the rice were neglected, the stench would be even worse.[79]

What if Haitians start speaking words of love and gratitude among themselves and over their country? It may seem too simple a strategy to induce development. However, it does work. I witnessed what love and gratitude can do.

A few years before passing away, my mom, Avenia, planted a

[79] Emoto, The Hidden Messages in Water.

Francique mango tree in her front yard in Petite Rivière de l'Artibonite. She took good care of it and spoke good words on it. Whenever I visited her, I would help water the mango tree and speak words of blessings over it. After a few years, the tree began producing large, juicy, and delicious mangoes. The fact that the mango tree was the only one of the four in the yard to produce fruit throughout the year was even more astounding. A year following my mom's passing, I asked my cousin Maurice if the mango tree was giving its fruit as usual. His response was a resounding "No. There is no such thing anymore." Gone the love, gone the exceptional fecundity.

Our words create our world. For too long, Haiti has been trapped in an environment where cussing, anger, and the use of force are signs of courage and strength. This dominant psychosocial trait may have flowed from the war strategy of the victorious former slaves. Because the war strategy culminated in a resounding victory, Haitians have come to believe that this strategy would produce success in times of peace. Thus, society has been tangled in Abraham Maslow's hammer syndrome. Resorting to cuss words, violent protests, a scorched-earth attitude, unending backward-looking, and superstition in the face of any issue only complicates and worsens the situation. Love, gratitude, and wisdom are the only lasting solutions.

Haiti is more of a concept than a geographical space because of its unequaled contribution to humanity. The time has come for Haitians everywhere to use this exceptionalism as a stepping stone and build on it with love, gratitude, and wisdom. They can start this development process immediately to bring deliverance and transformation to the country. Haitians owe it to themselves and the world to take the sunlit path to progress and development.

At the time of its independence, Haiti made a promise to the world. This promise sprang from victory over an incredible giant. This promise proclaims, "Anybody can overcome any challenge with an intense and burning desire to serve a legitimate and lofty cause." This promise also teaches that freedom is never free, but it is worth pursuing whatever the cost. Haiti delivered to the world a potent statement: "With freedom, men can fulfill their destiny, achieve lofty goals of progress and well-being, and live in a world of equality and fairness." Haiti also stated, "Freedom from external bondage leads to freedom from self-limitations and wants."

Since her independence, Haiti has strayed from her promises and statements into a barren wilderness of pride, division, and mismanagement. The time has come for the country to savor the taste of hope for a bright future. The year 1804 was not a finish line but a beginning. It is never too late for Haiti to bring to developing nations and poor people in the world a new message: "The wretched of the Earth can make it to the promised land of peace and prosperity." Haiti can renew its promise and become a bullhorn for the powerful master key from the Bible: "Love never fails; never stop giving thanks; and buy wisdom, education, insight." This master key will bring fresh hope to countless people by unlocking the gate to a peaceful, prosperous, and fulfilling life. Yes, Haiti can make the world dream again.

As Haitians navigate the complexities of personal growth, social development, and national reform, transformation will come through love, gratitude, and wisdom. The essence of a nation's renaissance lies in its people's hearts, rooted in love, fortified by gratitude, and guided by wisdom.

Love transcends all barriers and binds us together for a shared goal. It is the impetus for deeds of kindness, the cornerstone of resilient communities, and the foundation for long-lasting transformation. Gratitude, as a mindset of acknowledgment and appreciation, gives us hope and the ability to see the positive side of every circumstance. Knowledge and experience provide us wisdom, which lights our way and guides us in making choices that benefit society and individuals.

Haiti's past is replete with tales of bravery and tenacity. The nation has persevered through many hardships. We may avoid past mistakes with the help of love, gratitude, and wisdom. These principles sustain the reforms needed to create a wealthy and peaceful country. We must incorporate these principles into our culture.

They can give Haiti a fresh start and create a country that dreams and realizes its full potential—a Haiti where love never fails.

Love is a force that transcends all boundaries and permeates every aspect of our lives. It manifests in various forms: self-love, familial, community, and patriotic love, which are crucial in shaping our personal and collective identities. Self-love is the cornerstone of our wellbeing, which fosters our resilience and self-assurance. Love within the family strengthens the ties that bind together during good and bad times. Love for the community promotes cooperation and solidarity, which are essential for creating resilient and encouraging communities. Patriotic love encourages us to value, protect and serve our nation, driving us to support its development and well-being.

Love has been the impetus for numerous revolutionary movements and transformations throughout history. From Mahatma Gandhi's peaceful resistance to Martin Luther King Jr.'s Civil Rights Movement, love has demonstrated itself as a potent motivator for social change. These leaders used the force of love to bring people together, overcome obstacles, and establish equality and justice.

Haitians can express, nurture, and exhibit love in tangible ways daily. Little deeds of kindness, like lending a hand to a neighbor, volunteering at a nearby school, or just smiling at a stranger, can have a positive impact. Collaborating on projects, attending community meetings, and supporting neighborhood projects can all improve community ties and well-being. One effective approach to demonstrate affection for future generations is supporting education through donations, volunteer work, or lobbying for an improved system. Building a peaceful society requires embracing diversity and creating an inclusive atmosphere where everyone feels appreciated and respected.

Love, in all its forms, is a powerful and enduring force that has the potential to transform individuals, communities, and nations. By embracing and practicing love, Haitians can start saying a fraternal "I love you" to their compatriots, foster unity, and create a prosperous and peaceful country. According to the Holy Scriptures, "Owe no one anything, except to love one another, for the one who loves his neighbor has fulfilled the law. . . . Love does no wrong to a neighbor." (Rom 13: 8, 10)

Gratitude is a strong yet frequently underrated energy that significantly impacts individual and society development. It acknowledges and values all of life's blessings, no matter how minor. It is a way of thinking that helps us become more positive and content by turning our attention from what we lack to what we have. Cultivating thankfulness can be a life-changing practice in Haiti, where difficulties are common. It can help people and communities find strength in hardship. As a key component of personal empowerment, gratitude helps us develop a more positive attitude and improve our mental and emotional health by recognizing and valuing the good things in our lives. Gratitude promotes a cooperative attitude and improves social ties.

Community members' appreciation for one another's contributions creates an environment of mutual respect and support. This collective gratitude can be seen in the aftermath of natural disasters, where Haitians unite to rebuild their communities. Gratitude for shared efforts and resources strengthens ties and enhances resilience. Because individuals are more inclined to work together and support one another in societies where gratitude is prevalent, this attitude will cause initiatives like community gardens, cooperatives, and neighborhood support groups to thrive.

It is possible to develop gratitude by engaging in mindfulness.

Simple habits like writing down daily things for which one is grateful in a journal can significantly impact one's perspective and general well-being. Expressing gratitude to others helps strengthen constructive connections. Teaching kids to be thankful at an early age can help create a culture of kindness and appreciation in schools, setting the groundwork for a more empathetic and united community.

Haitians can strengthen and institutionalize gratitude to empower people and communities through programs that honor and promote community members' efforts. Similarly, incorporating gratitude into education can have a long-lasting, beneficial effect on society's well-being.

For its part, wisdom is the prudent use of information and experience to arrive at optimal choices. It is a quality that goes beyond intelligence alone and includes the capacity to perceive the broader picture, comprehend the complexity of human nature, and gracefully navigate life's challenges. Wisdom is crucial to the success of reforms and sustainable growth.

Wisdom is not limited to the domain of the intellectual elite. It serves farmers who are aware of the land's potential and its cycles, as well as senior citizens who have witnessed the highs and lows of life. It is the insight of young innovators who see a brighter future and the vision and courage of community leaders.

Wisdom entails pursuing policies that promote justice, equity, and the common good in governance. It requires knowledgeable leaders who possess the humility to listen to their constituents and the courage to make difficult decisions for the greater good. Historical figures such as Toussaint Louverture exemplify this blend of intellect and moral integrity. Drawing lessons from such leaders, we can cultivate a new generation of wise, compassionate leaders dedicated to national progress.

Wisdom is essential to resolving disputes and promoting peace. Servant leadership can heal divisions and promote reconciliation in a country with a social and political unrest history.

Establishing a peaceful society requires initiatives that foster communication, understanding, and collective problem-solving. By appreciating and considering the opinions of all parties involved, from local communities to government officials, Haiti may create a more harmonious and united society.

It is crucial to understand that wisdom, love, and gratitude make up a potent trio for transforming a country. Gratitude grounds us in humility and appreciation, love motivates us to act with empathy and compassion, and wisdom guarantees that our actions are deliberate and well-informed. Love, gratitude, and wisdom can build a strong foundation for the country's progress and a better future for all Haitians.

Practicing these principles offers a comprehensive individual and community development strategy, guaranteeing significant and long-lasting progress. Love gives us a sense of cohesion and purpose by motivating us to look out for one another and our country. Having gratitude makes it easier to recognize our accomplishments and those of others, which promotes a cooperative and upbeat atmosphere. Wisdom directs our activities, making sure that they are deliberate and informed.

These principles can be incorporated into national policies and initiatives to promote all-encompassing development. A national development strategy based on love, for example, would prioritize everyone's welfare and ensure that laws support social justice, inclusivity, and human rights. Initiatives encouraging volunteerism and community involvement can improve interpersonal relationships and a sense of shared responsibility.

Programs that honor accomplishments and acknowledge contributions can institutionalize gratitude. Distributing national honors and recognition to exceptional individuals, public servants, and community leaders can catalyze engagement and productivity. Education campaigns that encourage gratitude in the workplace and schools can foster a positive culture.

It is possible to integrate wisdom into governance by

encouraging open and responsible decision-making procedures. Long-term sustainability should guide the formulation of policies, striking a balance between social justice, environmental protection, and economic prosperity. Promoting public involvement in the formulation of policies can guarantee that a range of viewpoints are taken into account, resulting in more thorough and efficient solutions. Putting money into education that fosters ethical reasoning, critical thinking, and practical problem-solving can produce intelligent, capable citizens who can lead and innovate.

Haiti can establish a comprehensive and long-lasting route to peace and prosperity by incorporating love, gratitude, and wisdom into its culture. These principles guide us toward a future where every Haitian can prosper by enriching individual lives and strengthening the social fabric. Everyone feels appreciated and empowered when love propels our relationships, gratitude shapes our viewpoints, wisdom guides our decisions, disagreements become opportunities for cooperation, and obstacles become chances for personal development.

We must accept responsibility and take action to achieve our objective. Let's begin by supporting our communities, being kind to our neighbors, and practicing love in our families. Let's cultivate an attitude of gratitude every day by recognizing the contributions of others and enjoying the positive things in our lives. Let's strive for solutions that benefit everyone, learn from our mistakes, and make wise judgments. Let us treasure the conviction that love never fails. If we have love in our hearts, gratitude in our souls, and wisdom in our heads, we can create a Haiti that dreams and succeeds.

CONCLUSION

As we end our journey through this book, I encourage you to consider Haiti's many opportunities and challenges. We started by asking how Haiti may once again serve as a source of inspiration for the world and change its position from a place of suffering to one of rebirth and optimism. After studying Haiti's past and unbounded potential, it is evident that the Haitian people can dream and turn that dream into a reality.

I have highlighted the way forward by tackling Haiti's most pressing issues—poverty, social unrest, and institutional fragility—and pointing to the local and international resources that can effect long-lasting change. We have considered methods for social cohesion, economic empowerment, and institutional change based on the distinctive Haitian cultural traits. Still, without a shared commitment to action, none of this will materialize.

The future of Haiti rests on the vision and action of Haitians, both domestically and internationally, on leaders who prioritize the country's needs, and on collaborations with people who see Haiti's potential. It calls for a fresh perspective on leadership based on honesty, service, and humility. It demands a commitment to creating robust institutions that can bear the strain of accountability and the passage of time. And it requires having the guts to reconcile, heal, and move forward with a unified sense of purpose.

The question still stands: What should we do next? The answer is our willingness to be the change we want to see. The diaspora links Haiti and the rest of the globe, and it is in a position to bring resources, expertise, and passion, which are essential components of this new adventure. The diaspora's voices, skills, and tenacity will determine our country's course. And to Haiti's international allies, your encouragement and solidarity will help make the dream of Haiti's transformation a reality for everybody.

Let's envision a Haiti that emerges from the past with grace and strength, serving as an example of resiliency and self-determination. Let's imagine a country that appreciates each and every one of its citizens, where possibilities are available and hope is a daily reality rather than a far-off promise. As we move toward this vision, let us remember the essence of the Haitian spirit: unbreakable, courageous, and capable of inspiring the world.

Making Haiti a land of dreams again will not be easy. It will demand resolve, collaboration, and patience. However, if we cling to this vision and act with purpose, we can create a Haiti that supports every Haitian's aspirations and make the world dream again.

A new day of dreams come true is dawning on Haiti. Let us step into it together.

BIBLIOGRAPHY

Acemoglu, Daron, and James A. Robinson. Why Nations Fail: The Origins of Power, Prosperity, and Poverty. Reprint edition. New York: Crown Currency, 2013.

Acharya, Nish. "Mahatma Gandhi At 150: Lessons On Leadership." Forbes. https://www.forbes.com/sites/nishacharya/2019/10/02/mahatma-gandhi-at-150-lessons-on-leadership/.

"A/HRC/57/41: Situation of Human Rights in Haiti - Interim Report of the United Nations High Commissioner for Human Rights - Advance Edited Version | OHCHR." https://www.ohchr.org/en/documents/country-reports/ahrc5741-situation-human-rights-haiti-interim-report-united-nations-high.

"Les Rebelles: Contre l'ordre Du Monde: Mouvements Armés de Libération Nationale Du Tiers Monde (L'Histoire Immédiate) (French Edition): 9782020064132: Ziegler, Jean: Books."

"Basic Education for Young People and Adults, Ecuador - Effective Literacy and Numeracy Practices Database – LitBase." https://www.uil.unesco.org/en/litbase/basic-education-young-people-and-adults-ecuador.

Bluwal, Marcel, and Maurice Joly. Dialogue aux enfers entre Machiavel et Montesquieu. 1st edition. Paris: AVANT SCENE, 2018.

"Canciller de Venezuela Conmemoró El Aniversario 217 de La Independencia de Haití." https://conelmazodando.com.ve/canciller-de-venezuela-conmemoro-el-aniversario-217-de-la-independencia-de-haiti.

Carnegie, Dale. How to Win Friends & Influence People. New York: Pocket Books, 1998.

Cheibub, Jose Antonio. Presidentialism, Parliamentarism, and Democracy. New York, NY: Cambridge University Press, 2006.

Cicero, Marcus Tullius. How to Run a Country: An Ancient

Guide for Modern Leaders. Translated by Philip Freeman. Early Printing edition. Princeton: Princeton University Press, 2013.

Collier, Paul. "Haiti: From Natural Catastrophe to Economic Security," n.d.

CT.gov - Connecticut's Official State Website. "Declaration of Independence US Constitution." https://portal.ct.gov/sots/register-manual/section-i/declaration-of-independence-us-constitution.

Danticat, Edwidge. We're Alone: Essays. Minneapolis, Minnesota: Graywolf Press, 2024.

Derrida, Jacques. On Cosmopolitanism and Forgiveness. 1st edition. London: Routledge, 2001.

dpicampaigns. "Goal 1: End Poverty in All Its Forms Everywhere." United Nations Sustainable Development (blog). https://www.un.org/sustainabledevelopment/poverty/.

"Education for All in Haiti over the Last 20 Years: Assessment and Perspectives - UNESCO Digital Library." https://unesdoc.unesco.org/ark:/48223/pf0000136393.

"Education in Haiti." https://en.wikipedia.org/w/index.php?title=Education_in_Haiti&oldid=1273514688.

Ellis, Sebastian. "If the Only Tool You Have Is a Hammer, You Tend to See Every Problem as a Nail." The Fitzrovia Psychology Clinic, May 21, 2021. https://thefitzroviaclinic.com/if-the-only-tool-you-have-is-a-hammer-you-tend-to-see-every-problem-as-a-nail/.

Emoto, Masaru. The Hidden Messages in Water. Illustrated edition. New York: Atria Books, 2005.

Farah, Douglas. "HAITI'S TURBULENT BIRTH HAUNTS CRUMBLING FORTRESS." Washington Post, April 20, 1997. https://www.washingtonpost.com/archive/politics/1997/04/20/haitis-turbulent-birth-haunts-crumbling-fortress/fffd5179-6192-4d30-9fa2-b854613524dc/.

Ferrini, Luca. "The Importance of Institutions to Economic Development," n.d.

Fisher, Walter R. Human Communication as Narration: Toward a Philosophy of Reason, Value, and Action. Columbia, SC: University of South Carolina Press, 1989.

Frankl, Viktor E., William J. Winslade, and Harold S. Kushner. Man's Search for Meaning: Gift Edition. Gift edition. Boston: Beacon Press, 2014.

"From the Pulpit to the Heart | King's Last March | APM Reports." Accessed January 31, 2025. https://features.apmreports.org/arw/king/e1.html.

Fukuyama, Francis. State Building: Governance and World Order in the 21st Century: Governance and World Order in the Twenty-First Century by Francis Fukuyama (7-Jul-2005) Paperback, n.d.

"Funding of Political Parties and Election Campaigns: A Handbook on Political Finance | International IDEA." https://www.idea.int/publications/catalogue/funding-political-parties-and-election-campaigns-handbook-political-finance.

"Gal_country_profiles_haiti.Pdf." https://www.uil.unesco.org/sites/default/files/medias/files/2022/11/gal_country_profiles_haiti.pdf?hub=90.

Gallagher, Nancy Ambrose, Megan Eagle, Norma Sarkar, Silvia Cassiani, and Jody Lori. "Pan American Health Organization/World Health Organization Collaborating Centers in Nursing and Midwifery in Haiti." Revista Panamericana de Salud Pública 43 (March 15, 2019): e30. https://doi.org/10.26633/RPSP.2019.30.

Gide, Andre, and Alan Sheridan. The Immoralist. Translated by David Watson. Penguin Publishing Group, 2001.

Gordon, Eric A. "The 1802 Haitian Revolution on Stage: Liberty, Equality and Fraternity for All." People's World (blog), August 14, 2018. https://www.peoplesworld.org/article/the-1802-haitian-revolution-on-stage-liberty-equality-and-fraternity-for-all/.

"Grassroots.Pdf."https://www.oas.org/sap/docs/publications/grassroots.pdf.

"Gyges-a.Pdf."https://www.plato-philosophy.org/wp-content/uploads/2016/05/gyges-a.pdf.

"Haiti - Transparency.Org." https://www.transparency.org/en/countries/haiti.

"Haiti - United States Department of State." https://www.state.gov/reports/2022-country-reports-on-human-rights-practices/haiti.

"Haiti: Justice Reform and the Security Crisis | Crisis Group." https://www.crisisgroup.org/latin-america-caribbean/haiti/haiti-justice-reform-and-security-crisis.

"Haiti 'on the Verge of an Abyss', Warns UN Rights Chief | UN News." https://news.un.org/en/story/2022/11/1130182.

"Haiti_2012.Pdf." https://www.constituteproject.org/constitution/Haiti_2012.pdf.

"Haiti's Failed Truth Commission: Lessons in Transitional Justice - GSDRC." https://gsdrc.org/document-library/haitis-failed-truth-commission-lessons-in-transitional-justice/.

"Haiti's Troubled Path to Development | Council on Foreign Relations."https://www.cfr.org/backgrounder/haitis-troubled-path-development.

"Haiti:The Post-Revolutionary Period:1804-1820."http://faculty.webster.edu/corbetre/haiti/history/earlyhaiti/postrev.htm.

Hill, Napoleon, and Arthur R. Pell. Think and Grow Rich: The Landmark Bestseller Now Revised and Updated for the 21st Century. Revised&Enlarged edition. Québec: TarcherPerigee, 2007.

"How I Forgave the Man Who Murdered My Father | British Council." https://www.britishcouncil.org/voices-magazine/candice-mama-south-africa-forgiveness-reconciliation.

Howes, Lewis. The School of Greatness: A Real-World Guide to Living Bigger, Loving Deeper, and Leaving a Legacy. Reprint edition. Rodale Books, 2017.

"Les-Partis-Politiques-Dans-La-Construction-Haiti.Pdf." https://www.idea.int/sites/default/files/publications/les-partis-politiques-dans-la-construction-haiti.pdf.

"Literacy Rate by Country 2024." https://worldpopulationreview.com/country-rankings/literacy-rate-by-country.

"Message from Ms Irina Bokova, Director-General of UNESCO, on the Occasion of International Literacy Day: Literacies for the 21st Century, 8 September 2013 - UNESCO Digital Library." https://unesdoc.unesco.org/ark:/48223/pf0000222718_eng.

Morgan, Jacob. The Future Leader: 9 Skills and Mindsets to Succeed in the Next Decade. 1st edition. Erscheinungsort nicht ermittelbar: Wiley, 2020.

"National History Park – Citadel, Sans Souci, Ramiers - UNESCO World Heritage Centre." https://whc.unesco.org/en/list/180/.

"Nicaragua's Literacy Campaign - UNESCO Digital Library." https://unesdoc.unesco.org/ark:/48223/pf0000146007.

North, Douglass C. Institutions, Institutional Change and Economic Performance. 59262nd edition. Cambridge: Cambridge University Press, 1990.

"OAS :: Speeches." https://www.oas.org/en/media_center/speech.asp?sCodigo=15-0088.

Obama, Barack. The Audacity of Hope: Thoughts on Reclaiming the American Dream. First Edition. New York: Crown, 2006.

OBE, Lucy Brazier. ""'It Doesn't Matter Where You Came From. All That Matters Is Where You Are Going" Brian Tracy." Executive Support Magazine, January 31, 2019. https://executivesupportmagazine.com/it-doesnt-matter-where-you-came-from-all-that-matters-is-where-you-are-going-brian-tracy/.

"Occupation of Haiti (1915-34)." https://www.globalsecurity.org/military/ops/haiti19.htm.

"'Only Thing We Have to Fear Is Fear Itself': FDR's First Inaugural Address." https://historymatters.gmu.edu/d/5057/.

P4H Global. "5 Reasons Why You Should Care About Haiti's Independence Day (January 1st)," December 31, 2019. https://p4hglobal.org/p4h-blog/2019/12/31/5-reasons-why-you-should-care-about-haitis-independence-day-january-1st.

Price-Mars, Jean, and Magdaline W. Shannon. So Spoke the Uncle: = Ainsi Parla l'oncle. Washington: Three Continents Press, 1983.

"Prometheus."https://en.wikipedia.org/w/index.php?title=Prometheus&oldid=1272658757.

"Prononcé le 27 avril 2023 - Emmanuel Macron 27042023 Abolition de l'esclavage en France | vie-publique.fr," April 27, 2023. https://www.vie-publique.fr/discours/289309-emmanuel-macron-27042023-abolition-de-lesclavage-en-france.

"Reconciliation Must Evolve to Reflect Growing Complexity of Today's Conflicts, Participants Stress during Day-Long Security Council Open Debate | Meetings Coverage and Press Releases." https://press.un.org/en/2019/sc14024.doc.htm.

"Rfph_201802.Pdf."https://www.omrh.gouv.ht/Media/news/rfph_201802.pdf.

richardsh. "7 December 1965 Rabbi Abraham Joshua Heschel alongside Martin Luther King #otdimjh." On This Day In Messianic Jewish History (blog), December 7, 2015. https://jewinthepew.org/2015/12/07/7-december-1965-rabbi-abraham-joshua-heschel-alongside-martin-luther-king-otdimjh/.

Rojas, Don. "BATTLE OF VERTIÈRES: ITS SIGNIFICANCE IN THE LIBERATION STRUGGLE OF THE CARIBBEAN AND AFRICA." Caribbean Reparations Commission, December 8, 2020. https://caricomreparations.org/battle-of-vertieres-its-significance-in-the-liberation-struggle-of-the-caribbean-and-africa/.

Roldán, María Isabel Infante, and María Eugenia Letelier Gálvez. "La alfabetización de personas jóvenes y adultas en América Latina y el Caribe: análisis de los principales programas," n.d.

Rosalsky, Greg. "'The Greatest Heist In History': How Haiti Was Forced To Pay Reparations For Freedom." NPR, October 5, 2021, sec. Newsletter. https://www.npr.org/sections/money/2021/10/05/1042518732/-the-greatest-heist-in-history-how-haiti-was-forced-to-pay-reparations-for-freed.

Roumain, Jacques. Masters of the Dew: A Novel of Haiti. Liberty Book Club Edition. Libery Book Club, 1947.

Sagan, Carl. The Demon-Haunted World: Science as a Candle in the Dark (Paperback) - Common. Ingram International Inc, 2019.

"SECRETARY-GENERAL STRESSES NEED FOR POLITICAL WILL AND RESOURCES TO MEET CHALLENGE OF FIGHT AGAINST ILLITERACY | Meetings Coverage and Press Releases." https://press.un.org/en/1997/19970904.sgsm6316.html.

Smith, Matthew J. Red & Black in Haiti: Radicalism, Conflict, and Political Change, 1934-1957. https://academic.oup.com/north-carolina-scholarship-online/book/17598.

Socialist Worker. "Liberty and Equality in Haiti." https://socialistworker.co.uk/socialist-review-archive/liberty-and-equality-haiti/.

Soto, Hernando De. The Mystery of Capital: Why Capitalism Triumphs in the West and Fails Everywhere Else. Reprint edition. New York: Basic Books, 2003.

Stryker, Rod. The Four Desires: Creating a Life of Purpose, Happiness, Prosperity, and Freedom. New York: Delacorte Press, 2011.

"The African Nova Scotian Roots of Bob Marley's 'Redemption Song.'"https://www.thecanadianencyclopedia.ca/en/article/the-african-nova-scotian-roots-of-bob-marleys-redemption-song.

"The Myth of Daedalus and Icarus." https://www.greekmyths-greekmythology.com/myth-of-daedalus-and-icarus/.

"Tough Love Needed for Haiti | National Review." https://www.nationalreview.com/2010/01/tough-love-needed-haiti-jonah-goldberg/.

"Universal Declaration of Human Rights | United Nations." https://www.un.org/en/about-us/universal-declaration-of-human-rights.

venezueladmin. "Venezuela and Bolivia Celebrate Beating Illiteracy." Venezuelanalysis (blog), September 9, 2014. https://venezuelanalysis.com/news/10894/.

"Where Is the Wealth of Nations?: Measuring Capital for the

21st Century."https://documents.worldbank.org/en/publication/documents-reports/documentdetail/287171468323724180/where-is-the-wealth-of-nations-measuring-capital-for-the-21st-century.

INDEX

ABOUT THE AUTHOR

Jean Ricot Dormeus is a seasoned diplomat, author, and visionary leader devoted to the transformation of Haiti and the wider Americas. He has dedicated his life to international cooperation, peacebuilding, and integral development. His career spans decades with Haiti's foreign service and the Organization of American States (OAS).

JR calls Haitians to reconciliation, forgiveness, and a vision of shared prosperity rooted in love and honoring human dignity. He founded the Movement of Prayer for Haiti (MPH) and the Association of Haitians Living in Guyana (AHNIG), promoting spiritual growth, solidarity, and peace among his compatriots.

In his debut novel, Land of Dormant Dreams, and now in How Haiti Can Make the World Dream Again, JR combines policy wisdom, storytelling, and faith to chart bold paths toward national revival and global inspiration. His work is driven by a firm belief that Haiti's renaissance can spark hope and transformation far beyond its shores.

JR enjoys reading, writing, learning, playing the trumpet, tennis and golf, and supporting community development.

To connect with the author, visit:
https://jeanricotdormeus.com
jrdormeus@mphai.org

Made in the USA
Columbia, SC
07 June 2025

6d99f0fa-8cdf-42a2-bce1-be35017dbc39R01